Enjoy stirring up some memories of your own!

Deb O.

© 2018 by Deb Obermeier. All rights reserved.

Words Matter Publishing
P.O. Box 531
Salem, Il 62881
www.wordsmatterpublishing.com

No part of this publication may be reproduced, stored in a retrieval system, or transmitted in any way by any means—electronic, mechanical, photocopy, recording, or otherwise—without the prior permission of the copyright holder, except as provided by USA copyright law.

ISBN 13: 978-1-949809-26-8
ISBN 10: 1-949809-26-9

Library of Congress Catalog Card Number: 2019904627

CONTENTS

Dear Friends - by Aunt Mildred — iv

Acknowledgement - by Aunt Mildred — v

Preface — vi

January - All About Bare — 1

February - All About Seed Catalogs — 9

SPRING — 18

March - All About Back to Life — 19

April - All About A Day's Work — 27

May - All About Berries — 33

SUMMER — 42

June - All About the Garden — 43

July - All About Outdoors — 49

August - All About Apple Pickin' — 55

FALL — 62

September - All About Familiar — 63

October - All About the Pumpkin Patch — 71

November - All About Giving — 77

Winter — 85

December - All About the Perfection of Confections! — 87

Dear Friends,

    This is my recollection of recipes spanning generations. Many have been served and shared over the years with family and friends. It is my wish to keep them alive, presenting each with the same charm and grace with which they were first prepared and perfected.

    These jewels not only come from the recipes that I've gathered throughout my lifetime, but are also pieces of the past right out of Eliza's handed-down recipe box. Still sitting on the same shelf at Slipknot where Mimzie kept it displayed, just out of the reach of the kids but in clear sight to guide her through so many meals, its integrity remains intact.

    CJ feels honored each time Eliza tries one of his new creations, asking for a copy so she can add it to the collection, keeping the family history moving forward.

    Now, settled back in Spring Forrest with all of this history at my fingertips, it's my pleasure to keep these memories and creations alive. When the day comes that I'm no longer here to take the stage and tell the stories, it will be my secret comfort knowing that thumbing through these pages will do just that, simply stir up some of our fondest memories as we serve these familiar dishes.

                                                        Affectionately,

                                                        Aunt Mildred

Proudly added to the Simple Stitch Series

Acknowledgments

As you may have guessed by now, I had help gathering recipes and writing the reflections from Slipknot Farm and A Simple Stitch as well as CJ's Café. She goes by DebO and is very dear to me. You could say she is my hero, as she is the one that created me and gave me this wonderful opportunity to be a part of A Simple Stitch Series amazing journey. It's my understanding that she has plans to write a prequel when the series wraps up. I can't wait to see what my childhood was like in her imagination. But enough about me.

A little bird told me that growing up, DebO loved to cook and try her hand at baking any chance she got. Her mom came home and found a jar of egg yolks on the counter, and when she questioned where they came from, at 11 years old, DebO replied, "I'm making an Angel Food Cake from scratch. Is that ok?" She said her mom just laughed and replied, "We'll see."

Not only did the cake come out wonderful, but it was also just the beginning of her baking career. I understand she baked and decorated cakes for upwards of forty years. Wedding cakes were grand, and as the requests evolved, so did her style.

Holidays and family gatherings were so much fun to plan, paging through cookbooks and recipes collected along the way. Some were hand-me-downs from her family while some were finds in cookbooks that were tweaked to make a bit more pleasing. I understand DebO has a collection of cookbooks with notes in her handwriting in the margins dating back to the first time she prepared it. Many notes tell what the occasion was or where she took it. These have become family history books of sorts.

One of DebO's favorite recipes that has been baked and shared more than most is the Best-ever Chocolate Chip Banana Muffins. She happened upon this some years ago and immediately fell in love with everything about it. She has graciously shared this with the owner of Deb's Mugs and Muffins on Main Street right here in Spring Forrest, as it is affectionately served with the perfect blend of freshly roasted coffee beans and freshly brewed.

So, enjoy the following pages. As you prepare these favorites from A Simple Stitch Series, sparking memories from Slipknot or somewhere along historic Main Street, please feel free to make notes on my pages. Be certain to date and journal your special gathering or what urged you to try your hand at a new treat. After all, you never know, your cherished recipes may help a beloved character pen her own recipe book someday.

Remember, dream big, put a lot of effort in the things you do as to do them well and always, always use real butter! End every meal with a sweet-stopper!

Aunt Mildred

Preface

Welcome to A Simple Stitch. If you have never visited this quaint yarn shop on Main Street in Spring Forrest, I'm sure Eliza would be happy to invite you in. This lovely shop is all she ever dreamed of. It's where she entertains shoppers who quickly become friends and return time after time not only for yarn goods but a cup of coffee and a new story or two. Going upstairs to her apartment as she closes is like stepping back in time. She loves to stop at the window at the top of the stairs morning and night, taking a moment to gaze at the sky and count her blessings.

As for me, to everyone, I'm known as Aunt Mildred. I was on a journey across the country in my Winnebago taking my beloved husband Bill's ashes to the ocean. I had planned a visit in Spring Forrest. I hadn't seen family in a very long time. Needless to say, a turn of events during the holidays and my visit, thankfully, turned into a permanent stay. Settling back in Spring Forrest for good, I had no objections from Bill. He remains sitting quietly on the mantle of my charming home, just down the street from A Simple Stitch.

Spring Forrest has so much to offer. CJ's Cafe graces Main Street, just across the corner from A Simple Stitch. Something wonderful is always on the menu there. Up and down Main Street, shop after inviting shop you feel as if you have just stepped into Hometown U.S.A. and never want to leave.

Eliza has been blessed with Slipknot Farm, the old family Homestead from generations past, keeping it intact. She spends her free time in the country every chance she gets. There is always something going on in the kitchen. Whether it be heating a pot of left-over vegetable soup for lunch while taking in a Sunday visit or cooking for a gathering of sorts, the door is always open, and the oversized farmhouse work table is usually set to accommodate all who enter.

A Simple Stitch, A Common Thread affords you the pleasure of attending such a gathering. Set in the fall going into the holidays, the Homestead spills over with Faith, Family and Friends...and cooking! If you want inspiration or just a place to relax, A Simple Stitch, A Common Thread will certainly recharge your soul.

Followed by *A Simple Stitch, A Time to Mend,* we all know life isn't perfect. Summer is in full swing. Visitors return. The 'Girls Knit Out' group continue to gather on Friday nights. Main Street is bustling with visitors.

Although only six months after the holiday gathering, to some it seems an eternity. Life back to usual, the excitement has faded, and a sense of an unfamiliar emptiness takes over Eliza. She thinks I didn't notice. We all noticed! As Eliza plans a much needed weekend at Slipknot, an accident takes her by surprise. Changes are necessary, decisions are made without hesitation, and an unforeseen chain of events take place.

Finding a bit of intrigue on a new path for our dear Annie, the school teacher from Texas, unparalleled goals are brought to light in her relationship with CJ.

A Simple Stitch evolves when Eliza asks me to help out. This brought to surface my shop keeping memories and passion. Just as I thought, Slipknot Farm is certainly the place to be for working in the garden, cooking and finding rest while sitting on the swing and watching the sun set behind the barn. It does everyone a world of good.

As in every season, there comes change, and while not always easy, it can often be a true blessing in disguise.

I'm inviting you to find your own comfy spot in the sun and join us on our journey as you watch your garden grow.

I'm so excited to have you browse my recipe collection. Eliza was kind enough to share her recipe box that sits on the same shelf it has for generations at Slipknot. CJ let me in on some of his favorites from the Café, and I dug into my own collection as well.

I love making notes in my favorite books when I make a recipe for something special or tweak the recipe a bit to make it mine. Feel free to do the same throughout my pages. I certainly hope you find yourself returning time after time preparing new favorites with A Simple Stir while making Memories Served of your very own.

Be sure to let me know your new favorite. You can email my friend DebO at debobooks@yahoo.com! She will keep me posted!...wink, wink!

...and while you are waiting for your first batch of Butterhorns to come out of the oven, brew a cup of peppermint tea and start reading *A Simple Stitch, A Common Thread!* It is a perfect place to start!

                                                    Kindly,

                                                    Aunt Mildred

JANUARY—All About Bare!

    Once the twinkle lights go off for the last time and all of the all of the Christmas decorations are safely stowed away, doesn't the house seem even colder than just the onset of winter? I always thought so. Why do the holidays end just when winter is really beginning to set in?

    My way to offset these somewhat dreary days ahead is a good warm kitchen with something always simmering on the stove or baking in my oven. I've put together some of my favorites to help you through the weeks to come. If you are like me, you're probably in need of nourishment from the days of un-decorating you just conquered, as well! Soup's on!

Buttery Garlic Bread

Cheeseburger Soup

Great-Grandma's Potato Soup

CJ's Country Ham Scones with Maple Butter

Cream Puffs

Snickerdoodles & Chipper-doodles

Warming You Through Winter Lemon Cake

Buttery Garlic Bread

1 large loaf French bread
2 Tbsp. minced garlic
1/4 tsp. black pepper

1 c. butter
1 Tbsp. parsley flakes
1/2 c. parmesan cheese

Preheat oven to 375
Set aside 9 x 13 baking dish
Melt butter. Combine garlic, parsley and pepper in medium bowl with flat bottom.
Slice French bread into generous 1" slices.
Dip one side of bread into butter mixture. Stand in pan.
Continue to dip one side of each slice, standing plain side against dipped side in pan back into loaf form. Start new row with second half of bread.
If you run short on butter and garlic mixture, make more and continue.
Sprinkle with parmesan cheese and sesame or poppy seeds. Drizzle with any leftover butter mixture.
Bake uncovered for 15 minutes until heated through and lightly crunchy.
Serve immediately.

Cheeseburger Soup

This is a good, hearty soup that sticks to your ribs. On a day when I'm going to be working a bit harder than usual, I like to have this on hand. Fill up with a nice hot bowl of this, and I'm good to go for round two.

1 lb. ground beef
3/4 c. sliced carrots
1 tsp. parley
4 Tbsp. butter, divided
4 c. peeled, diced potatoes
1 1/2 c. milk
3/4 tsp. salt
1/2 c. sour cream

medium onion, chopped
3/4 c. chopped celery
2 bay leaves
*3 c. chicken broth
8 oz. American cheese
1/4 c. flour
1 tsp. black pepper

Brown beef. Drain and set aside.
In same skillet, sauté onions, carrots, celery and parsley in 1 Tbsp. of the butter until vegetables are tender.
Empty skillet into soup pot. Add broth, bay leaves potatoes and beef.
Bring to boil, reduce heat and simmer 10 - 15 minutes until potatoes are tender.
Remove bay leaves.
Meanwhile, in skillet heat remaining butter. Add flour, cooking 3 - 5 minutes until bubbly and golden.
Add to soup, bringing back to boil for 2 minutes to thicken.
Reduce to low, add cheese, milk, salt & pepper, stirring as cheese melts.
Remove from heat and stir in sour cream.
*3 cups of water with 4 chicken or beef bouillon cubes can be substituted for chicken broth.

Great-Grandma's Potato Soup

6-8 potatoes of choice, scrubbed, peeled and cubed
3 stalks of celery and tops, sliced
1 tsp. salt
1 tsp. pepper
½ tsp. celery seed.
6 c. water
3 chicken bouillon cubes
4 – 6 slices of bacon
3 Tbsp. reserved fat
1 large onion, sliced thin
3 Tbsp. butter
1/3 c. flour
1 c. half & half
2 slices American Cheese, if desired

Bring water, bouillon cubes, potatoes, celery, salt, pepper and celery seed to boil in large soup pot. Simmer until potatoes are tender.

Meanwhile, fry bacon until crisp. Drain on paper towel, set aside.

In same pan, drain all but about 3 Tbsp. fat and sauté onions in drippings until slightly browned. Remove the onions and set aside.

Melt 3 Tbsp. butter in pan with same drippings, add 1/3 cup flour, stirring and scraping until the flour begins to brown slightly.

Remove from heat and stir into pot with potatoes and broth. Return to heat and bring to a low boil, adding onions.

Reduce to simmer until mixture begins to thicken.

Stir in 1 cup half and half and heat just through. (If desired, add a couple slices of American cheese and stir in as it melts.

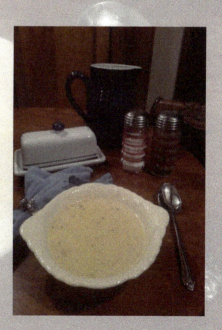

CJ's Country Ham Scones with Maple Butter

1-3/4 c. flour
2 tsp. baking powder
½ tsp. salt
¼ c. yellow cornmeal
2 Tbsp. sugar
¼ tsp. pepper
6 Tbsp. cold butter, cut up
¾ c. cook ham, slivered
1 c. whipping cream

Preheat oven to 425 degrees
Combine flour, baking powder, salt, pepper, cornmeal and sugar in bowl. Whisk to combine.
Cut in butter with pastry cutter until crumbly.
Stir in ham.
Add whipping cream, stirring with fork to combine.
Turn out on lightly floured surface and knead gently, 6 – 8 times to combine.
Place on lightly greased baking sheet. Pat into 7" circle.
Cut into 10 wedges. Do not separate.
Bake 25 minutes until lightly golden.
Cool slightly before separating.
Serve warm with Maple Butter

Maple Butter: Beat ½ c. softened butter, 2 Tbsp. maple syrup and 2 Tbsp. finely chopped pecans until fluffy and well blended.

Cream Puffs

Have you ever had a home-made cream puff? If not, you don't know what you're are missing out on! In the early days at the homestead, it was a real treat to have a stack of cream puffs with chocolate pudding and a stack of cream puffs with vanilla pudding gracing each end of the sideboard. Piled high and dusted with powdered sugar, one would not do. One of each was more like it. Give this a try, basic ingredients and a little time in the kitchen, your reward will be worth the effort and everyone will love you! Better yet, no one will ever forget you! Just ask Mimzie!

3/4 c. water   1/2 stick butter
1/2 tsp. salt   3 eggs
3/4 c. flour

Preheat oven to 400

Bring salt, water and butter to a boil in heavy saucepan.
Add flour, mixing vigorously with wooden spoon bring dough together, forming a ball. Cool to touch.
Add eggs, one at a time beating well, until smooth.
Drop by tablespoon onto cookie sheet.
Bake for 50 minutes.
Cool completely.
Carefully cut off tops, fill with pudding of choice and replace tops.
Dust with powdered sugar after arranging on large serving plate.

Snickerdoodles

Always a favorite of the kids, big and small, the gatherings always sported a gigantic jar of Snickerdoodles. Out of the blue one afternoon with the Homestead full of company, I remember Hank, the town handyman coming up to Eliza and as he complimented her on the get-together and fine meal he asked if he could offer a suggestion. Eliza was always open to new ideas. So from then on, adding mini chocolate chips to the Snickerdoodles and changing the name to Chipper-doodles became Hank's signature cookie! Every time he got the chance, he claimed the fame to the delicious go-to cookies with a little chocolate!

1 c. softened butter
1 ½ c. sugar
2 tsp. cream of tartar
¼ tsp. salt

2 eggs
2 ¾ c. flour
1 tsp. baking soda
¼ c. sugar & 2 Tbsp. cinnamon

Preheat oven to 400

Cream butter and sugar until fluffy. Add eggs.
Combine flour, salt, soda and cream of tartar.
Add to butter mixture to combine and form dough.
Take teaspoonful of dough, roll into a ball and roll in cinnamon/sugar mixture to coat. Place on ungreased baking sheet about 2" apart.
Bake 8-10 minutes until very lightly browned. Remove to wire rack to cool completely.
Makes about 6 dozen.

*For Chipper-doodles, stir in 1 cup mini chocolate chips into the flour mixture before adding to the butter mixture. Bake as directed.

Warming You Through Winter Lemon Cake

1 good yellow cake mix	3 eggs
1/2 c. butter	2 c. cold milk
1 1/4 c. water	1/3 c. sugar
2 – 4 oz. Lemon Instant Pudding	2 Tbsp. powdered sugar

Preheat oven to 350 degrees
Grease nice 9x9 baking dish or pan.
Prepare cake mix as directed on box. Pour in pan.
Place milk and water in large bowl. Add dry pudding mixes.
Beat with whisk for 3 minutes, blending well.
Pour over cake batter.
Place dish on cookie sheet, as may bubble over.
Bake 55 minutes, or until toothpick comes out clean.
Let stand in pan 20 minutes.
Sprinkle with powdered sugar.
Spoon into serving dishes. Serve warm.
May be garnished with fresh raspberries or fruit if desired.

FEBRUARY—All about the Seed Catalogs!

Although the shortest month, it seems to go on forever! The thoughts of spring pop into my head every morning when I rise and every evening when I turn off the lights and crawl in bed. That's why I look forward to the colorful seed catalogs that arrive almost daily. I make notes that turn to list that turn to this year garden plan.

Of course, when spring actually arrives, and I begin to clean up the remains of winter, my sore muscles convince me otherwise. So, I narrow my list to a favorite tomato plant, a packet of zucchini seed that I will plant only one hill and pass the rest along and then a trip to El & Em's Farmers Market for my favorite annuals and I'm all set.

But I must say, my February garden plan gets more elaborate with each passing year. Partly because I know I will never have to do the actual work! Here are some of my comfort recipes to enjoy while you make plans!

Sour Cream Coffee Cake

Eliza's Crowd-Pleasing Chicken & Noodles with Gnocchi

Smoked Pork Chops with Pepper Jelly Glaze

CJ's Calico Beans with Pineapple

Lilly's Beer Bread

Toasted Almond Fingers

Sour Cream Coffee Cake

Eliza has this Coffee Cake on the counter under a glass dome a couple of times a month. It gets moister as the days go by. She uses a heavy cast aluminum Bundt pan of sorts, presenting a cake that looks like something Mimzie would have made at the Homestead, and most likely, very well did.

Batter:
- 2 eggs
- 1/2 c. butter
- 1 tsp. pure vanilla
- 1 tsp. baking powder
- 1/2 tsp. salt
- 1 c. sugar
- 1-1/4 c. sour cream
- 2 c. flour
- 1 tsp. baking soda

Preheat oven to 350 degrees

    Grease and flour tube pan or Bundt pan and set aside.
    Cream eggs, sugar and butter until fluffy.
    Add sour cream and mix thoroughly.
    Place all dry ingredients in bowl and whisk to combine.
    Add to cream mixture, 1/2 at a time to mix well.

Streusel topping:
- 1/2 c. brown sugar
- 3 Tbsp. flour
- 3 Tbsp. butter
- 1/2 c. sugar
- 2 tsp. cinnamon

    Mix all ingredients until crumbly.
    Layer 1/2 of the batter evenly into pan. Top with 1/2 of the Streusel mixture.
    Top with remaining batter, then top with remaining Streusel mixture.
    Bake 50 - 60 minutes until toothpick comes out clean.
    Let rest in pan for 10 minutes.
    Turn out on plate. Immediately flip back on serving plate with Streusel topping upright.

Drizzle with glaze of 1 c. powdered sugar and 2 Tbsp. milk if desired.

*Blueberries, chopped apples, nuts or Craisins could easily be added to this recipe.

Eliza's Crowd-Pleasing Chicken and Noodles with Gnocchi

6 boneless chicken breast
4 chicken bouillon cubes
1 tsp. black pepper
1 medium onion, chopped
8 oz. carton portabella mushrooms
12 oz. bag wide egg noodles
2 Tbsp. cornstarch, dissolved In 2 Tbsp. water

8 c. water
1 tsp. celery seed
3 bay leaves
3 stalks celery, sliced
2 Tbsp. olive oil
16 oz. Gnocchi

Wash chicken, place in water with bouillon and seasonings.
Bring just to boil and reduce heat to simmer. Cover and let simmer good 30 – 45 minutes until chicken done.
Remove from broth to cool.
Chop into bite-size pieces when cool.
Meanwhile, wash mushrooms, remove stems and slice, then sauté in olive oil until golden brown.
Add onions, celery and continue to sauté to crisp-tender, 2 – 3 minutes.
Add to broth with slotted spoon, then bring broth back to boil.
Add noodles, reduce heat to slow boil and cook until almost done.
Add Gnocchi about 3 minutes before noodles are done and continue to boil until Gnocchi floats to surface.
By now noodles should be done.
Add chicken.
Reduce to low simmer, add dissolved cornstarch stirring constantly while broth thickens.
Remove bay leaves before serving.

Smoked Pork Chops with Pepper Jelly Glaze

A quick fix and all-time favorite for a evening meal is a batch of Smoked Pork Chops either grilled or simply baked in the oven for a short time. Oliver, often times prepares a batch when he has the grill nice and hot, so he has leftovers for the next few days. So simple and so tasty. Hope you get a chance to try them.

Desired number of Smoked Pork Chops

Pepper Jelly Seasonings to taste

To grill Chops, season to taste, coat top of chop with generous spoonful of pepper jelly.
Place on hot grill, let chop warm through and jelly set.
Turn and prepare top side same way. They don't have to grill long, about 10 minutes or so on first side, additional 5-8 minutes on second side, as meat is already cooked through.
To bake, season and coat each side of chop with pepper jelly.
Place in pan as desired.
Bake in 375 oven for 20-30 minutes or so, depending on number of chops and if overlapping in pan.
Check to see if heated through.
*A cup of apple juice or pineapple juice can be placed in bottom of pan if roasting.

CJ's Calico Beans with Pineapple

1-16 oz. can butter lima beans
2-16 oz. cans pinto beans
6 slices bacon, cooked and crumbled
¾ c. brown sugar
½ c. ketchup

1-16 oz. can red kidney beans
1-8 oz. can pineapple chunks
½ c. chopped onion
Tbsp. Dijon mustard
1 tsp. pepper

Preheat oven to 350 degrees.
Grease 5-quart Dutch oven or casserole dish.
Drain all beans. Drain pineapple, reserving juice and chop pineapple chunks.
Combine all ingredients. Pour into prepared dish, cover with lid or foil.
Bake for 1 hour.
Remove from oven, stir well, adding some of the reserved pineapple juice if beans look dry.
Return to oven uncovered and bake 15 minutes.

Serves 8-10

Toasted Almond Fingers

This recipe has become my signature cookie, making it since the early 80's for many occasions. They can be made with almonds but are just as delectable with finely chopped pecans. I prefer dark chocolate chips to dip these in, but they are not an overly sweet cookie, so milk chocolate works nicely as well.

Make all year round, just change sprinkles.

1 c. butter, room temp
¾ c. powdered sugar
1 Tbsp. milk
2 c. finely chopped almonds, toasted

2 c. flour
¼ tsp. salt
1 tsp. vanilla
6 oz. good chocolate chips

Preheat oven to 325 degrees
Cream butter and powdered sugar until fluffy, beat in milk and vanilla.
Add flour, salt and nuts to combine. Dough should come together and form a ball.
If too soft, chill for 30 minutes wrapped in plastic to prevent drying out.
Shape spoonful of dough into 2" fingers, placing on ungreased cookie sheet.
Bake for 15 – 18 minutes until very lightly browned.
Cool completely on wire rack.
Melt chocolate chips of choice in double boiler.
Dip one end about 1/3 of cookie, placing on waxed paper to set.
Sprinkle with desired sugars or decorations to compliment the season while chocolate is still soft.
Makes about 3 dozen cookies.

Lilly's Beer Bread

I must say, Lilly was a bit hesitant to share her Beer Bread recipe with Eliza, simply because she didn't know if beer was allowed at the Homestead. Oliver quickly came back from his cabin with 2 warm cans. He explained that he kept it on hand for company and Eliza just stood silent and grinned.

It has since been a welcomed addition to many a meal, as it is easy to make and oh so good. I'm sure Lilly will be pleased that I shared it with you as well.

2 ¼ c. flour   1 ½ tsp. baking powder

1 tsp. salt   3 Tbsp. sugar

1 can warm beer

Preheat oven to 375 degrees

Combine all dry ingredients in mixing bowl, stirring with whisk. Add warm beer, slowly pouring down side of bowl to minimize foaming. Mix well until incorporated.

Let stand for 15 minutes.

Pour batter in greased bread pan. Bake in preheated oven for 1 hour, brushing with melted butter after 45 minutes to brown.

Let cool in pan 10 minutes, turn out on wire rack and cool 10 minutes longer before slicing if serving warm.

(2 loaves can easily be baked at the same time without any adjustments, but mix each loaf separately)

SPRING

Always welcome. Long awaited. It is the time when the days begin to warm, the earth comes back to life and the promise of longer, sunnier days are a step closer. My favorite time!

Sometimes early, sometimes late, I have now learned how Easter Day is determined. Here goes. It is the first Sunday after the first full moon that occurs after the first day of spring! That's why Easter Sunday weather is so unpredictable for planning a family gathering and Easter egg hunt. Don't we just hate to cover up our Easter dresses with a coat? No matter what, we love the meal to follow!

Enjoy some of the favorites I have from Eliza's recipe box and if you have a chocolate pie lover in the family, wait until you see the Easter version I make!

Keep ingredients for soup on hand! There's nothing better on a chilly night or handier for a quick lunch. Especially on a sunny day when you are cleaning the winter out of your flower beds. I love to sit on the porch with a tall glass of iced tea and a bowl of soup and look at progress.

I save the not so warm days for spring cleaning. It never fails that I find a snow globe that escaped me when putting Christmas away. That just brings around another memory, another story and sometimes just the excuse I need to make another batch of Toasted Almond Fingers, this time with spring sprinkles of course!

Happy Easter! Happy Spring!

Aunt Mildred

MARCH—All About Back to Life

One morning when my feet hit the floor, I realize it isn't freezing anymore! It must be SPRING, glorious Spring! I can't get my first cup of coffee fast enough and head out to the porch. Of course, I always rush the seasons. Chalk it up to human nature.

As I take in the early morning air, it seems to renew my spirit from the inside out! Before I know it I'm in my yard flicking back leaves and looking for anything that may be starting to sprout, the slightest signs of anything remotely green makes me giggle. Suddenly I come to my senses, cover the tender vegetation over with the remains of winter and wait.

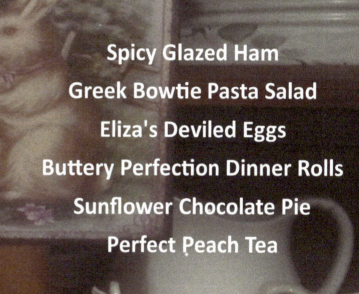

Spicy Glazed Ham

Greek Bowtie Pasta Salad

Eliza's Deviled Eggs

Buttery Perfection Dinner Rolls

Sunflower Chocolate Pie

Perfect Peach Tea

Celebrating Easter at Slipknot

No Easter Sunday would be complete without getting into the linen closet and finding a nice vintage tablecloth and an Easter basket to fill with a rainbow of colored eggs. It has been a lifelong tradition for me. I have carried this on even long after my kids were grown and had families of their own. It stirs the child in me. On occasion, I'm fortunate enough to have them home for an Easter visit, so then I don't feel so foolish.

The same goes for getting up extra early to be ready for the sunrise service at church. There's something about walking into the quiet church on Easter morning and watching the sunshine start to light the stained glass windows, almost as if God is slowly raising the shade to the darkness as we celebrate the resurrection. A season of miracles.

Since I've settled back in at Spring Forrest, I'm blessed with my extended family all about. Eliza always plans an Easter dinner with all the trimmings and Easter egg hunt to follow. Some years, we adults look pretty silly out there trying to remember where we hid those eggs when there are no children in the picture! One year, several weeks after Easter, Oliver brought me an egg he found by a bush when mowing at Slipknot! I had to be very careful not to break that one!

Speaking of breaking eggs, CJ was notorious for taking an Easter egg from the basket and cracking it on someone's head. I remember one Easter Eliza was going to teach him a lesson. She used a white crayon to write everyone's names on the eggs before dyeing them. Then the dye soaks into the shell except where the crayon wax is; you probably know that. Anyway, she dyed CJ's egg, raw! You can already see where this is going, can't you? And she waited. All day at Slipknot there was a trail to the giant common Easter basket she used as her centerpiece! Nearing the end of the day, doing a quick sweep for dishes, everyone was gathering up leftovers and taking their Easter goodies; CJ grabbed his egg. Just as Eliza turned to ask if anyone wanted to take any of the leftover Greek Pasta Salad, CJ popped her right in the forehead with his egg! All eyes on them, the room immediately went silent. I don't know who had the most shocked look on their face, CJ or Eliza! I'm pretty certain at one point CJ's brief, but colorful life may have flashed before him. What could Eliza say? With raw egg running down her nose and dripping off her chin, she was speechless. As Oliver passed by, he looked at Eliza, then turned to CJ and said, "next year, tell her you want your Easter eggs hard-boiled, those 3-minute eggs just don't do it!" He reached in the basket, grabbed a peep and sauntered out of the room. Eliza was the first to break the silence, and it wasn't long until the entire room was rolling! Now, that's an Easter we'll never forget! And like Jesus...he lived!

I have a nice assortment of our Easter recipes for you to try. They are favorites at Slipknot. Just a hint, you may want to save the deviled egg recipe for the week after Easter. A person can only eat so many hard-boiled eggs, and wear so many raw ones!

Enjoy!

Greek Bow-Tie Pasta Salad

Eliza made this lovely pasta salad one Sunday afternoon when we were opening up the Homestead at Slipknot. We sat out on the porch and enjoyed the lunch, the sunshine, and each other's company until the sun began to set. Since that time, it has become a favorite for Easter with a welcome assortment of colorful fresh vegetables and cheeses. Use what you have on hand, it always comes out perfect!

Spicy Glazed Ham

Ham of your choice and size for the occasion
Pepper Jelly (find recipe in index)
maraschino cherries
pineapple rings with natural juice
black pepper to taste
olive oil spray

Preheat oven to 325 degrees
Generously grease a Dutch oven or roaster to hold ham.
Place ham in prepared pan.
Drain pineapple juice from can over ham in pan.
Place pineapple rings on the ham in decorative pattern, securing with a couple of toothpicks, place maraschino cherry in center
Stir jelly to thin and spread over ham and fruit with either spoon or brush.
Sprinkle with black pepper.
Place in oven, covered with lid or foil. Bake for an hour or more, depending on size, to heat through.
Remove lid, add another coat of pepper jelly and spray ham and fruit with olive oil spray.
Return to oven uncovered for 30 minutes to caramelize the glaze.
Serve as desired.

Box of bowtie pasta
Good Greek Salad Dressing
1 large orange sweet peppers, cleaned & diced ½ red onion, thinly sliced
1 cucumber, stripe peeled, halved and sliced ½ c. sunflower seed kernels
2 c. assorted tomatoes in bite-size pieces
½ c. parmesan cheese
½ c. feta cheese, crumbled
small can black olives, sliced
Salt & Pepper to taste
1 tsp. celery seed

Cook pasta until tender. Drain and rinse again in cold water to cool down.
Drain completely, placing in large bowl and coat with Greek Salad Dressing to prevent sticking and clumping.
Drain black olives and add to pasta.
Prepare all vegetables and add to pasta. Mix well to coat, adding more dressing when needed.
Add both cheeses, sunflower seed, salt & black pepper and celery seed.
Combine well, adding Greek Salad Dressing to coat but not float!
Cover tightly, stir from time to time and chill completely before serving. Gets better second day.

Eliza's Deviled Eggs

Every family has the go-to person when it comes to bringing the Deviled Eggs! Ours is Eliza. Truth be known, she even has a collection of Deviled-Egg dishes, as well!

Hard-boiled eggs:

Start eggs in a single layer in enough cold water to cover them completely.

Turn on high heat and when the water comes to a boil, remove from heat and place lid on pot immediately.

Set timer for 15 minutes and do not remove lid.

When time is up, drain, fill with cold water rinsing until eggs are cool.

This yields the perfect egg, easy to peel and rarely a broken shell.

Peel eggs, rinse for shell bits and drain.

Slice each egg in half horizontally, pop out yoke carefully not to tear the white.

Take a fork and crumble yolks until no large lumps.

Add the following ingredients, adjusting amount for number of eggs:

Miracle Whip or mayonnaise

Dollop of sour cream

Spoon or two of sweet pickle relish with a bit of juice

Pinch or two of celery seed, bruised between fingers to release flavor

Kosher salt and coarse ground pepper to taste

Fill each egg dividing mixture evenly.

Sprinkle with Paprika for garnish. Chill.

Don't forget and leave them in the refrigerator, only to find when trying to put away leftovers after the meal…trust me, it happens!

Buttery Perfection Dinner Rolls

1 c. warm water (105-115 F)
2 packages active dry yeast
½ c. butter, melted
½ c. sugar
3 eggs
1 tsp. salt
4 – 4 ½ c. flour
3 Tbsp. butter, melted

Combine yeast in warm water to dissolve. Let stand until foamy, about 5 minutes.

Stir in butter, eggs and salt.

Add flour 1 cup at a time until dough gets stiff, all flour may not be needed.

Cover and refrigerate 2 hours up to 4 days.

When ready to use, grease 13 x 9 baking pan.

Turn chilled dough on lightly floured surface.

Divide dough into 24 equal-size pieces.

Roll each piece into a smooth ball, placing each in even rows in prepared pan.

Cover and let rise until doubled, about 1 hour.

Preheat oven to 375 degrees.

Bake until rolls are golden brown, 15 – 20 minutes.

Brush warm rolls with 3 Tbsp. melted butter, if desired.

Break apart to serve.

  Makes 2 dozen

Sunflower Chocolate Pie

I use my favorite pie crust recipe to make this. To me, the crust is my favorite part, but then, I've been known to roll out a pie crust, cut out shapes with a cookie cutter, sprinkle with cinnamon sugar and bake for a snack!...now back to the pie. Chocolate isn't always a springy look on the dessert table, but when you outline the edge of the pie plate with yellow chick marshmallow peeps, wing to wing facing toward the middle of the pie. Then you have the perfect Easter dessert!

Pie Crust of choice, baked and cooled. (It's Easter. Use a pretty pie plate!)

Filling:
1 ¼ c. sugar
¼ tsp. kosher salt
3 c. whole milk
1 ½ c. 60% cacao chocolate chips
2 tsp. pure vanilla extract
18 yellow marshmallow peep chicks
¼ c. cornstarch
4 large egg yolks
2 Tbsp. salted butter

Combine sugar, cornstarch and salt in medium saucepan, mixing well.
Add egg yolks and milk, whisking to mix well.
Cook over medium heat, stirring until mixture just starts to boil and thickens, 6-8 minutes, watching carefully.
As soon as starts to bubble and thicken, remove from heat.
Add chocolate, butter and vanilla and stir until everything is beautifully combined.
Pour into prepared pie crust and refrigerate until set. (about 4 hours)
Before placing on the dessert table, place peeps, facing into the pie, shoulder to shoulder spacing to accommodate the curve of the pie plate, to resemble a sunflower!

Perfect Peach Tea

Almost everyone at the Easter gathering loved my Peach Tea. It's nothing special, really, but sometimes I had to make the third pitcher before the day was over. I enjoy sun tea but March is too unpredictable, so I use my tried-and-true way to brew! That comes with a bonus in itself, as leaving the tea steep in the microwave for 10 minutes, the process steams up the inside really nice, so a wet cloth and a good wipe down, you have taken care of two task at once. Enjoy your tea, and you're welcome!

For two quart pitcher of tea, place a four cup glass measuring cup with three cups of cold water in the microwave. Place 2 family size tea bags in the water and four Country Peach tea bags in with them.
Set the microwave for seven minutes.
When time is up, glance to see when the ten minutes to steep will be up.
Remove the measuring cup with brewed tea, quickly wipe clean the microwave, and discard the tea bags, squeezing out the flavor against a spoon.
¼ cup of sugar is plenty to lightly sweeten this tea.
Serve over ice.

APRIL—All About A Day's Work

I love the warm days in April, several weeks into the season, I feel safe to remove the remains of the winter that has been protecting the new sprouts. Until now, I may peek, but gently cover them over, unsure of what the next few unpredictable weeks may bring.

Annuals are plentiful at every store and mulch is popping up in stacks on parking lots. Spring has sprung. Rule of thumb, speaking from experience, I vow to look but do not buy annuals until May 15th. Some years the weather makes it difficult to stick to that rule, but so many times, Blackberry winter will take them out or stunt the new plants so that they never show off that summer like you wanted them to.

For now, I will ramble around, cleaning out the remains of winter and drag out furniture, hose off the dust and arrange it in a new setting for this year. A fresh coat of paint to add a pop of the trending colors and my work is my reward. These days can be tiring, but the weekend after May 15th when I go out and buy way more annuals than I can plant in a day or two, I'm certainly thankful to have a comfy place to sit and admire my accomplishments. Won't you join me for tea?

Uncle Ben's Mile High Biscuits
Uncle Ben's Famous Sausage Gravy
Chicken, Rice and Black Bean Casserole
CJ's All-day Country Omelet
Best-ever Chocolate Chip Banana Muffins
GGG's Chewy Chocolaty Cookies

Uncle Ben's Mile High Biscuits

3 c. flour
4 tsp. baking powder
1 tsp. salt
3/4 c. butter or shortening
1 1/8 c. milk

Preheat oven to 475 degrees

Lightly grease 9x13 pan.
Whisk together all dry ingredients.
Cut in butter or shortening with pastry blender.
Add milk and blend lightly with fork until dough starts to come together.
Turn on lightly floured board and gently knead 30 seconds.
Roll or pat to 3/4 inch thickness.
Cut with biscuit cutter to desired size. Place in pan
Brush tops with melted butter if desired.
Bake for 12-15 minutes until golden brown.

Uncle Ben's Famous Sausage Gravy

1 lb. good pork sausage   1 tsp. ground black pepper
¼ c. butter   ¼ c. flour
2-3 c. milk

In large skillet, break apart sausage, add pepper and brown on medium heat until lightly browned and in small pieces.
Drain all but about 2 Tbsp. grease from sausage pan. Add butter and let melt over medium heat, careful not to burn.
Add flour, and combine with butter and sausage and spread out in skillet.
Watching carefully, stirring often, let flour cook and brown lightly in the butter.
Add 2 cups of milk, stirring to combine and bring sausage bits up from bottom of skillet, stirring constantly until mixture reaches a slow boil. Reduce heat and continue to stir as thickens.
Add more milk if necessary to get the gravy to the desired consistency.
Serve with Uncle Ben's Mile High Biscuits.
Great for leftovers, if lucky enough to have any left!

Chicken, Rice and Black Bean Casserole

2/3 c. lime juice
½ tsp. black pepper
1 tsp. garlic powder
4 c. cooked rice
2–15 oz. cans black beans
1 c. finely chopped cilantro
2 tsp. caraway seeds, crushed

1/3 c. olive oil
2 tsp. salt, divided
2 tsp. chili powder, divided
1 ½ lbs. boneless,
Skinless chicken breast
1 small onion, diced

Combine lime juice, oil, pepper, 1 tsp. salt, 1 tsp. chili powder and garlic powder, whisk well.
Add chicken and stir to coat evenly.
Place in plastic bag and refrigerate 2 hours.
In the meantime:
Grease 2-quart casserole dish.
Rinse and drain black beans.

Combine beans with rice, cilantro, 1 tsp. chili powder, 1 tsp. salt and caraway and diced onion.
Place in prepared casserole dish. Set aside.

Preheat oven to 350 degrees

Using a slotted spoon, place chicken in large, hot skillet, sautéing to cook until juices run clear. Do not overcook.
Stir into rice mixture and bake 45 minutes.
              Yields about 9 cups

CJ's All-day Country Omelet

2 c. frozen hash browns   5 eggs
¼ c. onion, diced   salt and pepper to taste
Olive Oil for sautéing   3 Tbsp. butter
½ c. shredded cheese of choice
Filling of choice: mushrooms, peppers, spinach, crispy bacon or ham.

To prepare crust:
Preheat oil in skillet, covering pan. Sauté onion until lightly golden.
Cover onions with hash browns, adding more oil if necessary. Fry until lightly brown, turning to prevent burning until potatoes are nicely golden and crispy.
While potatoes are frying, prepare additional fillings.
Beat eggs in bowl, adding a Tbsp. of water.
When potatoes are ready, spread in even layer in pan.
Carefully pour eggs over hash browns.
Add desired fillings, topping with desired cheese last.
Immediately cover with lid, reducing heat to prevent hash browns from burning.
After eggs are nearly set, place skillet under broiler to finish cooking and melt cheese. This is easier and will prevent potatoes from burning.
When set, loosen in skillet, folding half over and place on platter.
Top with additional cheese.
Serve as desired. Makes two nice size servings.

Best Ever
Chocolate Chip Banana Muffins

1 c. butter, melted	2 ¼ c. flour
1 ¼ c. sugar	¼ tsp. salt
1 large egg	1 tsp. baking powder
4 ripe bananas	1 tsp. baking soda
2 Tbsp. instant coffee	1 c. good dark chocolate chips

1 tsp. pure vanilla

Preheat oven to 350 degrees
Line 18-24 muffin cups with liners
Beat bananas, sugar and butter, blending well.
Add egg, instant coffee and vanilla. Mix until well combined.
In separate bowl, combine flour, salt, baking soda and baking powder, whisking to blend.
Add chocolate chips to flour mixture and whisk again to coat chips.
Turn mixer off, add dry ingredients at once.
Turn mixer on low and mix just to combine. Do not over blend.
Spoon into lined muffin cups, filling ¾ full.
Bake 22-24 minutes. Toothpick test for doneness.
Cool in pan. Store covered. Muffins get moister each day.

GGG's Chewy Chocolaty Cookies

1 ¾ c. butter	2 c. sugar
2 eggs	2 tsp. vanilla
2 c. flour	¾ c. good cocoa
1 tsp. baking soda	½ tsp. salt
1 tsp. inst. coffee	

1 c. dark chocolate chips, or chips desired

Preheat oven to 350 degrees.
Cream butter and sugar until fluffy.
Add eggs and vanilla.
In separate bowl, combine flour, cocoa, instant coffee, soda & salt.
Add to cream mixture. Stir in chips.
Drop by teaspoon onto ungreased baking sheets.
Bake 9 minutes. Do Not Overbake!
(They will puff during baking and flatten when cooled.)
Let cool on cookie sheet until flat, about 4 minutes then remove to wire rack to cool completely.

MAY—All About the Berries

From time to time when I walk into the kitchen at the Homestead, the large red stain on the wooden floor brings a smile to my face.

When Eliza's momma was but a young girl, she went berry picking one afternoon. Raspberries. Perfect for jam.

There was an old cook stove outside that was used for canning in the summertime in those years. Mimzie helped her cook down the raspberries to make a nice juice for the jam. After it cooled, she insisted that she wanted to carry the bucket in by herself.

The little stool that stood by the counter was hidden by the bucket she carried and in a blink, she went head over heels over the bucket and found herself sitting in a puddle of raspberry juice.

She was devastated, Mimzie was laughing hysterically at the scene, and for a long time, a pink apron and red stain on the wood floor reminded us all of that day. Now, after all those years, it still does.

I know Eliza loves to share the story every chance she gets. As for me, I just smile and listen to her tell it, knowing she is imagining her momma as a young girl, while she stands on the very spot she was sitting.

Raspberry Swirl Streusel Cheesecake
Fresh from Mimzie's Berry Patch Biscuits
Blackberry Scones with Blackberry Glaze
Miss Willamena's Blueberry Gateau
Blueberry Muffins CJ's Way
Chocolate Glazed Cheesecake Bites
Spring Blueberry Lemonade

Raspberry Swirl Streusel Cheesecake

The presentation of the Raspberry Swirl Streusel Cheesecake dims only to the wonderful aroma that fills the room when cooling and the combination of flavors that dance on your tongue when you take the first bite. This is always requested by Rachel every spring. Eliza gladly accommodates her, as she puts it, a little extra effort, but well worth it.

1 c. quick oats
1 c. flour
½ c. chopped nuts
2/3 c. sugar
1/3 c. whipping cream
¾ c. seedless raspberry jam

1 c. brown sugar
2/3 c. butter
3-8 oz. pkgs. cream cheese
¼ c. cornstarch
3 eggs

(Crust)
Mix together oats, flour and brown sugar. Cut in butter with pastry cutter until crumbly. Add nuts and mix in.
Place **all but 1 cup** of crumb mixture in a 10" springform pan, lightly greased. Press into bottom and up sides. Place on baking sheet.
Bake at 350 degrees for 18 minutes until set.

(Filling)
In mixer bowl beat cream cheese, sugar, cornstarch and cream until smooth.
Add eggs and beat on low speed 5 minutes, scraping bottom and sides of bowl.
Pour into baked crust.
Place jam in bowl. Stir vigorously to thin. Place by spoonful on top of cheesecake.
Take butter knife and swirl through the batter, careful not to disrupt bottom crust.
Reduce heat to 325 degrees, place back on cookie sheet and bake for 1 hour 15 minutes.
Remove from oven, spread remaining cup of crumbs evenly over top of cake and immediately return to oven and bake 15 minutes.
Turn off oven and let cheesecake sit in oven for 30 minutes.
Remove, cool an hour, release sides and remove from pan onto serving plate.
Chill overnight.

Fresh from Mimzie's Berry Patch Biscuits

2 c. bread flour
½ c. sugar
¼ tsp. coarse salt
2 eggs, slightly beaten
2 Tbsp. water
1 Tbsp. sugar
2 Tbsp. milk or cream
1 ¼ c. powdered sugar

2 c. cake flour
2 Tbsp. baking powder
1/3 c. cold butter
*1 c. buttermilk
2 c. fresh blackberries or red raspberries
½ tsp. pure vanilla
mint leaves for garnish

*substitute 1 tsp. vinegar and milk to make 1 cup, let stand 5 minutes.

Preheat oven to 350
Grease large baking sheet and set aside.
In favorite large mixing bowl, add flours, ½ cup sugar, baking powder and coarse salt, whisking to combine.
Cut in cold butter until mixture is crumbly, using pastry blender.
In small bowl mix together eggs, buttermilk and water.
Make well in center of the flour mixture and add liquid all at once.
Using a fork, stir just to moisten, making a dough.
Turn dough out onto a lightly floured surface, kneading gently 4-6 turns, or just until dough holds together nicely.
Roll into a ½ inch thick circle. Cut 8 rounds with biscuit cutter or favorite round shaped cookie cutter 2 ¼ inch round. Place on prepared baking sheet about 2" apart.
Cut 8 more rounds with 2 ½ inch cutter if possible, or same cutter if none available, re-rolling dough as necessary.
Set aside 8 berries. Top biscuits on baking sheet with remaining berries, then sprinkle with 1 Tbsp. sugar. Top with remaining dough rounds.
Bake 30-35 minutes until golden brown. Cool on wire rack for 15 minutes.
Meanwhile, combine 3 Tbsp. cream, vanilla and stir in enough powdered sugar to make a glaze. Drizzle over biscuits and top each with reserved berry and mint leaf to garnish. Serve warm.

Blackberry Scones with Blackberry Glaze

2 c. flour
¼ tsp. baking soda
½ c. butter
¼ c. milk

1/3 c. sugar
¼ tsp. cinnamon
1 egg, slightly beaten
1 c. frozen blackberries

Preheat oven to 450 degrees
Combine flour, sugar, baking soda and cinnamon in mixing bowl.
With pastry blender, cut in butter until pea-size.
Add milk and egg, mixing with wooden spoon until well blended.
Gently, fold in the blackberries.
Turn out on lightly floured surface and pat into a 1-1/2" thick round. Cut into 8 wedges and place on ungreased baking sheet.
Bake until lightly browned, about 15 minutes. Remove to wire rack to cool.

Glaze:

1 Tbsp. butter
1 Tbsp. heavy cream
1 tsp. vanilla

2 large blackberries
1 c. powdered sugar

Combine butter and 2 berries in bowl and heat or microwave until soft. Mash berries and add heavy cream.
Add powdered sugar and vanilla, stirring to make glaze. Add more cream if mixture too thick.
Drizzle over scones and serve.

36

Chocolate Glazed Cheesecake Bites

These amazing treats are the perfect accessory to a lovely bowl of fresh berries, of any kind. I loved to surprise everyone at a Sunday afternoon meal by setting out the big crock of berries and a spoon. They all looked at each other as if to say, surely there's a shortcake or biscuit or cookie of sorts to go with them? As I brought out the pile of Cheesecake Bites, stacked elegantly on a special pedestal serving plate, I always got a standing ovation and round of applause. Right crowd, someone would even whistle. So worth the effort!

Crust:

2 c. graham cracker crumbs
1/2 tsp. salt
8 Tbsp. butter, melted
1/2 c. powdered sugar
1 tsp. cinnamon

Filling:

3-8 oz. pkg. cream cheese, room temp.
1/2 c. heavy cream
1 Tbsp. pure vanilla extract
1-1/2 c. sugar
4 large eggs, room temp.
1 tsp. fresh lemon zest

Glaze:

2 c. good quality dark or milk chocolate chips
2 squares vanilla almond bark or desired sprinkles

Preheat oven to 375 degrees
Line 9x13 pan with foil, extending ends over ends and fold down for easy removal. Spray lightly with cooking spray.
For crust, stir together crumbs, sugar, salt and cinnamon.
Add butter to combine and press in bottom of 9x13 prepared baking pan.
Bake 10 minutes just to set.
Remove from oven and set aside while filling is being prepared.
To prepare filling, combine cream cheese and sugar, mixing on low speed until smooth.
Add cream, eggs, vanilla and zest, mixing on low speed, scraping down sides and bottom. Continue to mix on low speed for 3 minutes.
Spoon filling into prepared crust, smooth.
Reduce oven temp to 325 degrees. Bake 35-40 minutes until set.
Cool in pan 30 minutes. Cover and place in refrigerator until cooled completely, at least 2 hours.
When ready to start glazing process, lift cheesecake from pan onto cutting board.
Carefully cut into approximate 2" squares, placing on cookie sheet, slightly separated.
Place in freezer 30 minutes while glaze is being prepared.
For glaze: Melt desired chocolate in top of double boiler, stirring occasionally until smooth.
Working quickly, dip each slightly frozen cheesecake square in glaze to coat, dripping off excess. Place on wax paper lined cookie sheet to set.
If desired, melt the vanilla almond bark or sprinkles of choice, drizzle or decorate and place in refrigerator to completely set chocolate glaze.
To store, when chocolate completely set, stack in container with tight lid and store in refrigerator until served. Makes 24 bars

Spring Blueberry Lemonade

2 pints blueberries
1 ½ c. sugar
1 ½ c. fresh lemon juice
1 ½ quarts spring water
fresh mint
peach slices for garnish

Process berries, sugar and lemon juice in food processor until smooth.
Strain through a fine sieve into pitcher and stir in spring water.
Serve over ice, garnished with fresh peach slices and mint if desired.

Makes about 2 quarts

Miss Willamena's Blueberry Gateau

1 c. flour	1 tsp. baking powder
½ tsp. salt	½ c. butter, softened
1 c. sugar	2 large eggs
2 ½ c. fresh blueberries	1 Tbsp. powdered sugar

Preheat oven to 350 degrees

Lightly grease 9" springform pan and dust with flour.
Place flour, baking powder and salt in bowl and combine with whisk.
Beat butter and sugar in mixing bowl until fluffy.
Add eggs, one at a time and continue to beat.
Reduce speed and add flour mixture, mixing just until incorporated.
Spread batter in prepared pan.
Toss blueberries in 1 Tbsp. sugar and 1 tsp. flour, coating berries evenly.
Spoon berry mixture over batter, almost to the edge.
Bake on middle rack of oven, placing pan on cookie sheet or pizza pan.
Bake 1 hour.
Cool on rack. After cool, loosen sides and transfer to serving plate.
Dust with powdered sugar.

Blueberry Muffins CJ's Way

2 c. flour

1/2 c. sugar

1 Tbsp. baking powder

1/2 tsp. salt

1 tsp. cinnamon

1/2 c. milk

1/2 c. butter, melted

2 eggs

1 tsp. pure vanilla

1 1/2 c. fresh or frozen blueberries

Preheat oven to 425 degrees

Line cupcake pan with 12 liners

Combine dry ingredients in large bowl and set aside.

In mixing bowl, combine butter, eggs and vanilla.

Toss blueberries into dry ingredients to coat berries.

Stir butter mixture gently into dry mixture with berries to combine.

Fill cups. Sprinkle tops of muffins with additional sugar-cinnamon mixture before baking.

Bake 15 minutes.

41

SUMMER

When this season rolls around my thoughts, turn quickly to 'home-grown tomatoes' fresh from the vine and still warm from the sun. Nothing compares. Our meals are planned around a plate of sliced tomatoes, a sandwich built around these bright slices or a salad that wears them well.

Then as the squash start to bloom and produce, my meals change gears. There is so much we can do with these fresh vegetables. Some of the best recipes in Eliza's recipe box came from Mimzie's early years of abundance. Fried, grilled or baked in a bread, what's not to like about zucchini?

As the story goes, each year anxiously waiting to start her garden, that first day out, she would over-do it. Nose to the ground she would tear in, working like there was no tomorrow. The problem was the plants and seeds seemed so small, it was easy to see how Mimzie miss-judged the harvest to follow.

My memories of gardening bring to mind the muscles that hibernated all winter. The next morning was a challenge for me to stand up out of my comfy bed. On the bright side, the soreness gave me the perfect excuse to sit in the sun and take in what I had accomplished the day before.

This year, I think I will use Eliza's idea and make a scarecrow to keep me company while working in my garden of 2 tomato plants and a hill of zucchini. Perhaps I will dress her in some vintage clothes to remind me of Mimzie in her early years. Keeping good company and reminiscing of days gone but not forgotten make easy a good day's work. I believe I will add a row of marigolds around the edge of my tiny garden, and a sunflower or two, just for fun!

JUNE—All About the Garden

When I think of the garden, it brings to mind memories Mimzie shared with me so long ago. She depended on the garden to feed the family, and on a good year, she was able to share with those less fortunate. Mimzie possessed a natural curiosity to try new plants and seeds. She certainly learned a valuable lesson the summer she put out a dozen hills of zucchini squash. She not only perfected the way she prepared fried zucchini but she was happy to share her recipe with anyone who would take a basket or two of the abundance.

As I was looking through Eliza's recipe box, I found the directions she had written out in her own handwriting, on a scrap of paper, yellowed from age and a few stains from constant use.

Next year, if you get over-anxious with zucchini, please, feel free to use Mimzie's idea and share your harvest and her recipe. I added a few of my own recipes as well because one can never have too many ways to use zucchini! Enjoy!

Deep Fried Zucchini

Mushroom Cilantro Bites

Cabbage Patch Soup

Papa's Fried Cabbage and Noodles

Pepper Jelly

Aunt Mildred's Lattice-Topped Rhubarb Pie

Lemon Melon Coolers

Deep Fried Zucchini Squash

Adjust the ingredients for the amount of squash you will be fixing. Heat oil to 375 degrees and use a good canola or vegetable oil. Great for mushrooms as well.

You will need flour, seasonings, eggs, milk and well-seasoned bread crumbs.

Rule of thumb: for 2 medium-size zucchini, you will need about 2 cups flour, seasonings desired, 3 eggs, ¼ cup milk, 3 cups breadcrumbs (I use seasoned breadcrumbs), oil for deep frying.

Wash and dry the squash, slice thinly, about 1/4" thick. Set aside.

In a container with tight-fitting lid, add flour and seasoning salt, coarse black pepper, Chipotle or Red Pepper if you want some heat, or season as desired. Mix to combine.

Place sliced zucchini in flour mixture, secure lid and shake to coat well.

In medium bowl, mix eggs and milk, beating well.

Place breadcrumbs in bowl or pan, suitable for dredging. Oil should be pre-heating at this point.

With meat fork, take zucchini coated in flour, dunk to coat in egg mixture, place in breadcrumbs, use hand to pile breadcrumbs on top of zucchini, then press gently to help hold, shake off excess and place on plate.

Place layer of squash at a time in fryer basket, or pan, and fry until golden brown, turning if necessary, 3 – 5 minutes.

Remove from oil, placing on cookie sheet with cooling rack to drain, standing squash in rows as they cool. Salt to taste.

Cabbage Patch Soup

1 lb. ground beef
4 ribs celery, chopped
1 medium onion, chopped
2 c. water
1 – 16 oz. can white navy beans, drained and rinsed
1 – 14 oz. can stewed tomatoes or fresh stewed tomatoes
4 c. shredded cabbage
1 tsp. pepper
1 tsp. chili powder
1 tsp. salt
2 c. hot mashed potatoes
½ c. grated parmesan cheese

Brown beef in large soup pot. Drain.
In same pot, add onion, celery, salt and pepper.

Cook 5 minutes.

Add remaining ingredients except mashed potatoes and cook until cabbage is just tender.
To serve, top each bowl of soup with a scoop of hot mashed potatoes, sprinkle generously with grated parmesan cheese if desired.

Mushroom Cilantro Bites

Who would have ever guessed that there would be a bumper crop of Cilantro of all things, in an herb garden! Well, Uncle Oliver sent bundles to CJ at the Café to "work his magic with" as he put it, and CJ did just that! These bites are just as good right from the oven, room temperature or cold on the way out the door in the mornings. Give it a try; you might want to double up on this recipe.

2 Tbsp. butter & olive oil
½ small onion, chopped
1 lb. button mushrooms, sliced
4 eggs
¼ tsp. ground nutmeg
¼ c. fine breadcrumbs
½ c. minced fresh cilantro
1 c. parmesan cheese
salt & fresh ground black pepper
2 c. shredded Monterey jack cheese

Preheat oven to 325 degrees. Butter an 8" square baking dish.

In large pan over medium-high heat, add 2 Tbsp. butter and olive oil mixture.

Add the mushrooms and onions, cooking to release moisture and brown lightly, about 10 minutes, stirring often. Add nutmeg. Season with salt, pepper to taste and set aside.

Beat eggs with fork, then stir in bread crumbs, cilantro, 1 ½ cups of Monterey jack cheese and ½ cup parmesan. Add mushroom mixture and combine well.

Pour into prepared baking dish and bake 30 minutes, just until set.

Sprinkle with remaining cheeses and return to oven. Bake 5 minutes just until cheese melts. Remove and cool on rack about 15 minutes, just until cool enough to cut.

Cut into 1" squares, arranging on platter.

Papa's Fried Cabbage and Noodles

This is a great one pan quick fix that can be used as a side dish or served as a meal. A piece of cornbread and you're set. Perfect for one of our busier days at the Antique Store so many years ago. To me, it's comforting to fix when I'm feeling a bit sentimental. My kids have shared with me that they do the same thing from time to time. Hopefully, you will enjoy it as much as we do.

Large head of cabbage,
½ c. chopped onion
Sliced, then roughly chopped
1 tsp. celery seed
½ lb. of bacon
Medium wide egg noodles
salt and pepper to taste

Prepare egg noodles according to package directions, drain.
In large heavy skillet, brown bacon. Remove to drain on paper towels.
In same skillet, sauté onion until begins to brown.
Quickly add all of the cabbage, stirring to combine with onions.
Add celery seed, salt and pepper.
Place lid on skillet and turn heat to medium-low to cook cabbage without burning. Stirring cabbage from time to time, lift lid and allow water from steam to drain into skillet to steam cabbage. Do not overcook. Should only fry about 5 minutes.
Remove from heat, stir in prepared egg noodles.
Crumble bacon and stir in just before serving.
*Use your judgment as to the amount of bacon drippings you leave in the skillet before you start to fry the onions. Remove some if too much grease.

Pepper Jelly

Be sure not to make the same mistake I did the first time I made several batches of the colorful, wonderful tasting jelly. I thought it would be perfect for Christmas gifts if I covered the lid with a square of Christmas print and secured it with a tag held by a piece of jute cord. I thought of adding a jingle bell, just to be more festive! As my mind wandered, my hands soaked up the juice from the bowls of peppers I cleaned and seeded, preparing to chop in the food processor. That was the last time I cleaned any peppers without gloves. My hands were tingling as if on pins and needles well into the night. Take my hard-learned advice, add rubber gloves to your list when you get ready to make this jelly!   Aunt Mildred!

2-3/4 c. finely chopped assorted peppers   1-1/2 c. cider vinegar
1 Tbsp. crushed red pepper flakes, if desired   6-1/2 c. sugar
1 pouch (Certo) liquid pectin

Use an assortment of peppers; colorful mixture works best. Add jalapenos to desired strength, cleaning and removing seeds from all. Peppers may be chopped in food processor.
Have clean sterilized canning jars and lids ready.
Combine all ingredients except Certo in heavy pot, bringing to rolling boil that cannot be stirred down.
Add Certo, return to rolling boil, and boil for 1 minute, stirring constantly.
Remove from heat and carefully fill jars, wiping rim of jar and seal Immediately.
Cool, and check to be sure each lid sealed.
As each jar seals, the ping coming from the kitchen is like a 'well done' calling out a reward for the efforts.

Aunt Mildred's
Lattice-topped Rhubarb Pie

Use your favorite pie crust recipe for this, making enough for a two-crust pie. I have always been partial to a lattice-topping. This lets the ruby red of the rhubarb peek through. It can easily be topped with a rolled crust and a cute design cut out with cookie cutters or slits. Your call, your creation. No doubt everyone will rave about the taste!

Pastry for Two-Crust Pie
2 lbs. rhubarb, trimmed, rinsed and cut into 1" pieces
1-1/2 c. sugar
¼ c. cornstarch
1/4 tsp. pure orange extract
1 tsp. grated orange zest

Prepare crust following your favorite recipe.
In large bowl combine the sugar, cornstarch, orange zest and orange extract, mixing this very well.
Add rhubarb, tossing to combine completely.
Preheat oven to 400 degrees.
Prepare bottom crust in 9" pie pan.
Place filling in the prepared crust, mounding high.
Top with lattice crust, or desired design. If making lattice, roll out crust same as bottom crust, and using pizza cutter, cut entire crust into 1" strips. Weave crust over top of filling, then fold bottom crust and crimp, pressing in the ends of lattice as you go.
Spray with olive oil spray, lightly, and sprinkle with sugar.
Bake on cookie sheet or pizza pan for 50 – 60 minutes until bubbly. Cool on wire rack.

Lemon-Melon Cooler

2 c. lemonade
3 c. seedless watermelon
1 c. ice cubes

Place all ingredients in blender, cover. Blend on high speed until smooth.
Serve in favorite chilled glasses with melon balls & lemon slice on skewer for garnish if desired.
SERVES 4

JULY—All About Outdoors

Summertime is in full force. I remember the excitement of the fourth of July celebration. Everyone gathered at the park. There was a carnival in town. Fireworks that evening just at dusk, about the same time the mosquitos swarmed in for a snack. But who noticed? The focus was on the sky.

After that, days swimming and playing with friends, sometimes even a summer camp kept us entertained for a week or so. We were never bored. We were always hungry.

After my children were enjoying their summers off, we had a mid-week picnic at the park. Several of the families on the adjoining blocks joined in. It became an unspoken ritual every Wednesday afternoon. Blankets strewn on the ground, checked tablecloths on the picnic tables and an endless row of picnic baskets, as if set up as a grand buffet was found at the same shelter weekly. What memories were made by children and adults alike.

I hope during this mid-summer month you have the opportunity to make and share some memories with your neighbors and friends. You won't regret it. Those picnic baskets are always filled with the best food!

If you are lucky enough to find a park with a creek you can even cool off with an evening swim. Drench the kid in you! I still do, every chance I get. We never outgrow the fun of a good picnic!

Eliza's Simply Superb Chicken Salad

CJ's Cafe Special Zucchini Patties

Eliza's Crunchy Cole Slaw

Banana Cupcakes

Easy Oatmeal Fudge Drop Cookies

Summertime Frozen Ambrosia Pie

Eliza's Simply Superb Chicken Salad

6 chicken breast, bone in
½ tsp. salt and 1 tsp. pepper
1 tsp. celery seed
1 medium onion, diced
½ c. Craisins, chopped
½ c. sliced almonds crushed
½ c. Miracle Whip or mayo
reserved broth

3 chicken bouillon cubes
3 bay leaves
1 Tbsp. parsley flakes
3 ribs celery, diced
½ c. sour cream
4 oz. cream cheese

In large pot, place clean chicken breast with enough water to cover completely. Add salt, pepper, celery seed, bay leaves, parsley and chicken bouillon. Bring to boil and reduce temperature immediately to simmer, cover and let cook 20 – 30 minutes or until chicken is done and tender.
Let cool in broth. If making ahead, remove chicken from bone, place back in broth and refrigerate overnight.
Remove chicken from broth, cut into small chunks.
Onion and celery can be chopped in food processor if desired.
Place Craisins in food processor, pulsing to chop.
Place cream cheese, sour cream and Miracle Whip in food processor, pulsing to blend, drizzling about ¼ cup reserved chicken broth into mixture. Additional ½ tsp. salt and ½ tsp. pepper and ½ tsp. celery seed may be added to mixture if desired.
Mix all ingredients thoroughly, adding a drizzle of broth to get a good consistency.
Cover well and chill for at least an hour for flavors to blend.
Serve as desired.

CJ's Café Special Zucchini Patties

3 medium zucchini, finely diced
1 Tbsp. parsley or cilantro
2 Tbsp. parmesan cheese
olive oil for pan frying
2 eggs, beaten
1/2 c. flour
salt & pepper to taste

Line cookie sheet with paper towels. Spread with diced zucchini and sprinkle with 1/2 tsp. salt. Let drain 30 minutes.
Combine zucchini, eggs, parmesan cheese, flour and parsley or cilantro.
Season to taste.
Batter should be thicker than pancake batter.
Heat 2" oil in heavy skillet to hot.
Spoon very generous Tbsp. full of batter into oil.
Reduce heat to medium, fry 2-3 minutes until golden, turn and fry another 2-3 minutes until golden.
Drain on rack while frying remaining patties.

Eliza's Crunchy Coleslaw

There are often request for Eliza's Coleslaw. If you like a bit of sweet and tart, you will enjoy this different combination.

16 oz. bag coleslaw mix
3 – 3 oz. pkgs. Ramen noodles
4 green onions, diced
1 c. sliced almonds
½ c. sunflower kernels
½ c. vegetable or canola oil
6 Tbsp. white vinegar
¼ c. sugar
1 tsp. salt
1 tsp. pepper

Combine oil, vinegar, sugar, salt and pepper in pint jar. Shake well to combine.
Place in refrigerator, shaking every 10 minutes or so.
Combine coleslaw mix, green onions, almonds and sunflower kernels in large bowl.
Break Ramen noodles into pieces, saving the flavor packet for use another time.
Stir Ramen noodles into the coleslaw mix to combine well.
About 30 minutes before serving, add dressing mixture to coleslaw mix and combine well.
Stir well again before serving.

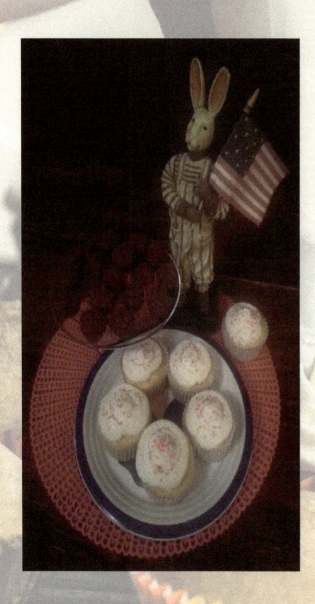

Banana Cupcakes

I know. You are thinking 7/8 cup melted shortening? Really? Well, I have never tried it any other way, and I don't know how that measure came to be either. The trick I learned if you have a concern about that measure, melt a cup of shortening, remove 1 Tbsp. and there you go. Exactly 7/8 cup! It's well worth the trouble. This also makes up a nice 9x13 cake as well. It's really yummy!

3 ripe bananas, about 1 ½ c.	2 c. sugar
7/8 c. melted shortening (Crisco)	2 eggs
*1 c. buttermilk	1 tsp. baking soda
1 tsp. baking powder	2 ½ c. flour
Pinch of salt	1 tsp. pure vanilla

Preheat oven to 350 degrees

Line muffin tins with paper and set aside.
Beat bananas and sugar on low speed until smooth.
Combine buttermilk and baking soda, let stand to dissolve.
Whisk together flour, salt and baking powder.
Add buttermilk mixture, flour mixture, shortening, eggs and vanilla to banana mixture, beating on low only until mixed.
Bake 15 – 18 minutes, until toothpick comes out clean.
Frost with favorite icing.

*Substitute buttermilk with 1 tsp. vinegar and enough milk to make 1 cup. Let stand 5 minutes.

Easy Oatmeal Fudge Drop Cookies

2 c. sugar
½ c. milk
6 heaping Tbsp. cocoa
3 c. oats
1 Tbsp. peanut butter
1 stick butter
1 tsp. pure vanilla
½ c. coconut

Line 2 large cookie sheets with waxed paper. Set aside.
In saucepan, bring sugar, milk and cocoa to a boil.
Boil for 1 minute, stirring constantly.
Remove from heat, add peanut butter and vanilla.
Mix well.
Add oats and coconut immediately, stirring to combine.
Drop by spoonful on waxed paper to set.

Summertime Frozen Ambrosia Pie

1 Prepared graham crust
1 – 8 oz. can crushed pineapple
1 – 14 oz. can sweetened condensed milk
¾ c. toasted flaked coconut
2-1/2 c. frozen whipped topping, divided.
1 – 11 oz. can mandarin oranges
1 – 8 oz. package cream cheese

Drain oranges and pineapple, reserving 2 Tbsp. of pineapple juice.
Gently press oranges and pineapple between paper towels to remove excess juice.
Beat cream cheese until fluffy.
Add pineapple juice and condensed milk until smooth.
Fold in 1- ½ c. of the frozen topping (thawed).
Gently fold in oranges and pineapple and coconut.
Spoon into crust, forming nice surface on top of pie.
Cover with plastic and freeze until firm.
Before serving, let stand at room temperature about 20 minutes.
Garnish with dollop of remaining whipped topping, add maraschino cherry and pecan half if desired.

AUGUST—All About Apple Pickin'

How excited I was to be invited along to El & Em's in the peak of apple season. Oliver wanted to get some to share with Jon and have on hand at Slipknot, so I thought I would pick a few for myself. Spending as much time at A Simple Stitch as I do now, a nice basket of apples on the counter to share would be perfect.

The thing is, you know how you put a pot on the stove with good intentions to make a small pot of soup or chili for supper and perhaps enough for leftovers the next day, then you continue adding ingredients until the pot is full to the rim? We all tend to do that. Who would have thought a nice wicker basket in an apple orchard would work the same way.

Getting my basket of apples to the truck took both Oliver and myself to carry, hanging on to a handle on each side. Every apple I spotted looked perfect, ripe, juicy and in need of picking! And so I did.

Luckily I like apples, have time in the evenings and found a bunch of family favorite recipes. The best part will be gaining popularity when I start delivering these goodies to everyone I know. Apple Butter anyone?

Aunt Mildred's Apple Crisp with a Twist

Aunt Mildred's Perfect Apple Cheesecake

Autumn's Harvest Apple Cake

Cinnamon-Apple-Raisin Cookies

Apple Pecan Pull-Apart Bread

Aunt Mildred's Apple Crisp with A Twist

4 c. apples, cored and sliced,	1/3 c. sugar
1/3 c. brown sugar, packed	¼ c. butter
1/3 c. flour	1 tsp. cinnamon
¾ c. oats tossed	½ tsp. pure vanilla
¼ c. finely chopped nuts	½ c. Craisins or raisins

Preheat oven to 350
Lightly grease either 9" square pan or deep dish pie pan.
Toss oats and vanilla together in small bowl and set aside.
Prepare apples, peeling if desired, cut in quarters, remove core and slice thinly in uniform slices, toss with the 1/3 cup of sugar.
Place in pan.
In medium bowl, combine brown sugar, flour, oats, nuts and cinnamon.
Add butter and work in with fork or fingers to form a crumble.
Sprinkle evenly over apples to cover completely.
Bake for 30 minutes until lightly browned.

Serve warm or cool completely.
This can be made with berries in season or any other fruit suitable for baking. Mix peaches and blackberries for a special mid-summer treat. Serve with a scoop of favorite vanilla ice cream! Yummy!

Aunt Mildred's Perfect Apple Cheesecake

I love to put a little extra effort in the dessert when I'm having company or for a special occasion. Honestly, this cheesecake takes very little effort but looks like it was made by a professional pastry chef. So when you want to 'wow' them or just present a lovely dessert, this would be the recipe! It tastes as good as it looks!

(Crust)
3/4 c. butter   1/4 c. sugar
1 1/2 c. flour   1/2 tsp. vanilla

Beat butter until fluffy. Add sugar, flour and vanilla.
Mix until dough forms ball.
Press into the bottom and up sides of an ungreased 9-inch springform pan.
Place in the refrigerator while preparing filling.

(Filling)
2- 8 oz. cream cheese   1/4 c. sugar
2 eggs   3/4 tsp. pure vanilla

Beat cream cheese and sugar until fluffy.
Add eggs and vanilla. Beat to mix thoroughly.
Pour evenly into crust. Return to the refrigerator.

Preheat oven to 350

(Topping)
3 c. thinly sliced apples   1/4 c. sugar
1 tsp. cinnamon

Combine cinnamon and sugar.
Toss together with apples.
Arrange over filling starting on outside edge, laying in circles to cover top of cheesecake.
Place on cookie sheet or pizza pan and bake for 55-65 minutes or until set.
Cool on rack for an hour. Run knife around inside of pan and release the sides of the pan.
Remove the bottom of the pan by sliding a knife under cake to release. Place on serving dish. Store in refrigerator

Autumn's Harvest Apple Cake

1 2/3 c. flour   ½ c. sugar
1 ½ tsp. baking powder   2 eggs, beaten
¾ tsp. salt   3 c. apples, diced
¾ c. butter   1 c. chopped nuts
Sugar for dredging

Preheat oven to 350 degrees.
Stir flour, salt and baking powder in large bowl.
Rub in butter until resembles coarse crumbs.
Stir in sugar, fold in apples and nuts. Stir in eggs with metal spoon until thoroughly amalgamated.
Scrape batter in 8" deep cake pan.
Bake 50 minutes or until toothpick comes out clean.
Cool in pan 10 minutes, then unmold onto wire rack.
Cool 30 minutes.
Dredge top with sugar and serve warm.

Cinnamon-Apple-Raisin Cookies

1 1/2 c. apples, cored, peeled and chopped
1 c. cinnamon chips
1 c. raisins
1/2 c. chopped nuts
1 1/4 c. brown sugar, packed
1/2 c. butter, softened
2 eggs
1/4 c. milk
1 1/4 c. flour
1 1/2 tsp. cinnamon
1 tsp. baking powder
1 tsp. salt
1 c. oats

Preheat oven to 400

Place apples, chips, raisins and nuts in a bowl, mix well.
In mixer bowl, beat brown sugar and butter until creamy.
Add eggs and milk, mixing well.
Whisk flour, cinnamon, baking powder and salt together. Stir into butter mixture.
Blend in the fruit and nut mixture. Add oats.
Drop by Tbsp. full 3 inches apart onto a parchment lined baking sheet.
Bake for 8-10 minutes until set and lightly browned.
Cool on sheet 5 minutes and remove to wire cooling rack to cool completely.
*Butterscotch Chips may be substituted for Cinnamon Chips

Apple Pecan Pull-Apart Bread

2 apples, cored and chopped
1 c. pecans, chopped
*2 cans biscuits
1 stick butter
1/3 c. brown sugar
1/2 c. sugar
2 Tbsp. cinnamon

Preheat oven to 375 degrees.
Generously grease heavy Bundt pan or tube pan.
Melt butter.
Place brown sugar evenly over bottom of pan.
Sprinkle with half of the apples and pecans.
Drizzle half the melted butter over combination.
Cut each biscuit into 6 pieces. (use either pizza cutter or scissors for ease)

Combine cinnamon and sugar in large bottom bowl. Toss biscuit pieces a dozen or so at a time in cinnamon mixture and layer in pan over apples and pecans.
After first can used, layer remaining apples and pecans on dough and drizzle with butter.
Continue to layer second can of biscuits in same fashion until used.

Sprinkle with cinnamon sugar mixture left over.
Bake for 20 - 25 minutes until golden and when pieces on top tapped or lifted, not doughy underneath.
Let stand in pan 5 minutes. Carefully turn out on serving plate, watching for running juices.
Serve warm or cool.

*Double batch of biscuit dough works well. Just pinch off pieces and drop into cinnamon sugar mixture.
**This is also good with raisins or Craisins added to nut and apple mixture.

FALL

Isn't autumn's beauty a testimony of the simple grace of God? The trees are sporting every color imaginable, showing off, while the sunlight dances on their leaves as if to say, "Look around you at the abundant beauty that our audacious God has blessed us with."

When I get up, the early mornings require heavy socks and a soft throw while I sip my first cup of coffee on the porch, contemplating what this glorious day will bring. Getting dressed, I slip into fall clothes of vibrant colors and fabrics a bit heavier for the early hours, but not unbearable when the sunshine once again warms the day as this amazing season engulfs me.

As the crisp breeze crosses my face, I embrace the chill on my cheeks. As I breathe in, the air speaks to my soul, as if refreshing and renewing my spirit.

It won't be long until the smell of wood smoke and burning leaves fill the air. Later on that evening, we will build a campfire to warm us and play with our senses as we all sit huddled together, watching sparks dance into the night sky.

Take time out to embrace the transformation of this amazing season and all of the gifts it brings...and toast a marshmallow or two...just because!

SEPTEMBER—All About Familiar

As the days begin to get shorter and we feel the change in the air, it seems like our nature to hold on to the past. Some of us reach deep into our memories, and it's amazing the comfort that can be found in a dish someone made for us upon request again and again, even though it was not as amazing as we remember. We embrace that fuzzy feeling, don't we? I want to share some of those recipes that bring back these feelings. Perhaps it will remind you of something from days gone by that did the same for you. Enjoy with a happy heart.

Sunday Morning Early to Rise Coffee cake

Annies' Favorite Southwest Lasagna

Mama Simpkins Prize-winning Gourmet

Texas Sheet Cake

GGG's Unforgettable Pineapple

Upside-Down Cake

Calico Pepper Cornbread with Pepper Jelly

Mimzie's Fried Chicken

Sunday Morning Early to Rise Coffee Cake

To get everything ready before church on Sunday mornings, it required getting up a bit earlier. This wonderful yeast coffee cake takes a bit of time to rise, but having the warm, old-fashioned treat for breakfast helped to make you shine at Sunday service. If there were any leftovers, they were just as good for a snack later in the day.

1 package dry yeast, soaked in ½ cup warm water
1 c. warm milk
½ c. sugar
1 egg, slightly beaten

1 tsp. coarse salt
¼ c. shortening
4 c. flour

Additional sugar and cinnamon for topping and butter to drizzle on dough.

Mix all ingredients except flour to combine.
Add 4 cups flour, mixing well.
Place in greased bowl, turning once to coat. Cover with towel and let rise in warm spot until double, taking about 30 minutes.
Punch down. Divide dough in two equal pieces. Place evenly in 2- 9" baking pans, cover with waxed paper and let rise again, taking about 15 minutes.
Sprinkle cinnamon sugar on top of dough and drizzle with melted butter.
Bake at 375 degrees preheated oven for 15-20 minutes until lightly brown.
Although this is not a very detailed recipe, it is easy to perfect with a little practice. It's never hard to find volunteers to help get rid of extras!

Annie's Favorite Southwest Lasagna

In the fall while growing up in Texas, at least once a month Annie would request her favorite supper and her dad, Jon, was the only one she thought could do it up right! Now when she really starts to miss him, she told me that she would try the dish herself. Of course, there were leftovers for way too long, and it never tasted the same. I'm anxious for her to request it from him this fall. Everyone wants a taste of Texas on a cool evening at Slipknot. Think I will tag along in the kitchen when he does. I love to watch a cowboy cook!

2 lbs. ground beef
1 - 15 oz. can enchilada sauce
1 - 3 oz. can sliced black olives, drained
1 tsp. minced garlic
1 ½ c. small-curd cottage cheese
8 - 8" corn tortillas, halved
1 c. shredded cheddar cheese

1 medium onion, chopped
1 – 14 oz. can diced tomatoes
1 tsp. salt
1 tsp. black pepper
½ lb. Monterey Jack cheese, thinly sliced
1 egg

Generously grease your favorite 13x9x2" baking dish. Set aside.
In large skillet, brown ground beef and onion. Drain well.
Stir in enchilada sauce, tomatoes, olives, salt, garlic and pepper.
Reduce heat and simmer for 20 minutes.
In mixing bowl, combine cottage cheese and egg. Set aside.
Preheat oven to 350 degrees.
Spread one-third of the meat sauce in the prepared dish.
Top with half of the Monterey Jack cheese, half of the
cottage cheese mixture and
layer half of the tortilla pieces to cover.
Repeat layer, ending with remaining third of the meat sauce.
Cover with cheddar cheese.
Spray foil with cooking spray and cover.
Bake 20 minutes.
Uncover and bake additional 15 minutes until cheese bubbly.
Let stand 10 minutes before serving.

Calico Cornbread with Pepper Jelly

2 boxes Jiffy cornbread mix   2 eggs
1 c. sour cream   ½ c. milk
½ c. three color sweet peppers, chopped
¼ c. melted butter
¼ tsp. red pepper, if desired
1 Tbsp. sugar

Preheat oven to 400 degrees
Grease desired small baking pan or iron skillet or pie plate.
Mix all ingredients to combine well.
Spread evenly in pan.
Bake 15 -20 minutes until done, depending on depth of pan.
Serve warm with butter and pepper jelly.

Mimzie's Fried Chicken

whole fryer, cut up
2 tsp. salt
good oil for frying

2 c. flour
1 tsp. pepper

Wash chicken and pat dry.
Combine flour, salt and pepper in shallow dish or pie pan.
Dredge chicken in the flour mixture to coat well.
Heat about 2 inches of oil, canola or vegetable oil, in heavy skillet with tight-fitting lid.
When oil hot, place chicken in pan, put on lid and reduce heat to medium.
Let fry for 10 - 15 minutes or so, until almost golden brown.
Remove lid, careful not to let water from steam fall into oil. Turn all pieces, replace lid and let this side fry for 10 - 15 minutes until golden brown.
Lift lid, tilting to let water collected from steam run into skillet and quickly replace lid.
Continue to fry on medium to low heat 15 - 20 minutes longer, tilting lid to drain water into skillet several times. (when water cooks away you will see the oil starting to fry the chicken again, then tilt lid to steam again)
Remove chicken to platter when done.
*Mimzie used a tiny pickle fork to turn the chicken. It had a little red knob on the end and only two tiny prongs. She said that was the secret to her amazing fried chicken. I believe her!

Momma Simpkins Prize-Winning Gourmet Texas Sheet Cake

I remember so clearly the night that Miss Annie Simpkins came in to join the Girls Knit Out one Friday evening. She had made her momma's prize-winning Gourmet Texas Sheet Cake as a thank you for her first trip out to Slipknot. She was a nervous little thing and just rambled on and on. Now, Annie is one of the gang, always present and a part of Spring Forrest. We sure wish she would bring us another one of those cakes!

Did I mention, Annie has the blue ribbon she won that year at the fair!

Cake:
- 2 c. flour
- 2 c. sugar
- 2 large eggs, room temperature
- ½ c. sour cream or buttermilk
- 1 tsp. vanilla
- 1 c. water
- 2 tsp. instant coffee
- ½ tsp. salt
- 1 tsp. baking soda
- 2 sticks butter
- 4 Tbsp. very good cocoa
- ½ c. seedless raspberry jam

Preheat oven to 350 degrees.
Generously grease a 10 x 15 jelly roll pan and set aside.
Combine flour, sugar, eggs, salt, sour cream, baking soda and vanilla in mixing bowl. Mix well to combine. Set aside.
In saucepan, melt butter, cocoa, instant coffee and water to combine. Bring to a boil, then add all at once to the flour mixture. Mix well.
Pour batter into greased pan, smoothing out evenly.
Bake in preheated oven for 20 - 25 minutes.
Remove from oven when toothpick comes out clean, let rest 5 minutes and immediately brush with Seedless Raspberry Jam that has been stirred vigorously with a spoon to thin.

Fudge Icing:
- 1 stick butter
- 6 Tbsp. milk
- 1 tsp. vanilla
- 4 Tbsp. very good cocoa
- 1 lb. powdered sugar
- 1 tsp. instant coffee

Heat butter, cocoa, instant coffee and milk in heavy saucepan.
Bring to a boil, stirring constantly.
Remove from heat, stir in powdered sugar and vanilla.
Spread immediately on hot cake.

When completely cool, pipe caramel or melted chocolate in lattice design or drizzle over cake. Sprinkle with toasted sliced almonds and give a slight dusting of cracked sea salt to knock some of the sweetness if desired.

GGG's Unforgettable Pineapple Up-Side-Down Cake

We all have someone that turned something ordinary into a special treat for any occasion. This was it for our family. Simply made, turned out on a cookie sheet. Nothing fancy. Absolutely mouthwatering. When we want to remember GGG fondly, we either talk about her up-side-down cake, or if time permits, try and make one just like she did. Memories! Enough said!

1 good yellow cake mix
1 stick butter, melted
3 large eggs
5 Tbsp. butter

1 large can pineapple slices,
in juice, drained & reserved pineapple juice & water to equal 1 c.
1 c. brown sugar
maraschino cherries

Preheat oven to 350 degrees
Generously grease 9x13 baking pan.
Whisk together cake mix, 1 cup pineapple juice (& necessary water), 1 stick melted butter and eggs. Batter should be smooth.
Melt the 5 Tbsp. butter. Dump in pan. Cover bottom of pan with brown sugar.
Carefully arrange pineapple slices to cover bottom of pan.
Place maraschino cherry in center of each slice.
Pour batter over spatula to carefully cover all pineapple slices. Smooth top.
Bake 30 minutes or until toothpick comes out clean.
Let stand 5 minutes.
Invert onto cookie sheet, or desired platter.
Scrape leftover brown sugar glaze from pan and add to top of cake.

69

OCTOBER—All About the Pumpkin Patch

I remember back in the day, pumpkins were plentiful and not used only for decoration. Mimzie taught me to cut the pumpkin in half, seed it and place it cut side down on a baking pan and roast in a 300-degree oven for an hour or so, softening enough to make it easy to peel.

The pumpkin was cooked down and made into pumpkin butter, much like apple butter or simply canned for use later.

Seeds were salted and roasted to be used as a garnish or snack.

I'm happy to share some of the recipes Eliza kept as well as some of CJ's creations he wanted to share. After all, who doesn't love this amazing gourd called the great pumpkin! (I know Linus would agree.)

Caroline's Abundant Harvest Squash Soup

Annie's Surprise Dinner-in-a-Pumpkin

Sweet Potato Biscuits

It's a Pumpkin - No! It's a Cheese Ball

Pumpkin Cranberry Coffee cake

Orange-Pumpkin Cookies

Caroline's Abundant Harvest Squash Soup

2 medium carrots, sliced   2 ribs celery with leaves, chopped
1 medium onion, chopped   ¼ c. butter
2 lb. butternut squash, peeled and seeded, then cubed, about 6 c.
4 c. chicken stock or broth   ½ tsp. salt
½ tsp. ginger   ¼ tsp. pepper
½ c. half & half

Sauté carrots, celery & onion in butter for 10 minutes until tender.
Add prepared squash, broth and ginger. Bring to a boil.
Reduce heat and simmer about 25 minutes until squash is very tender. Set aside and cool to room temperature.
Mash with potato masher in small batches, or use food processor to puree in small batches, until smooth.
Return to pan, heat through, adding half & half, salt & pepper. Do not boil.
Garnish with Roasted Pumpkin Seeds, or chopped pecans if desired.

Annie's Surprise Dinner-in-a-Pumpkin

1 medium pumpkin   4 c. hamburger, browned
1 tsp. pepper   1/4 c. soy sauce
2 Tbsp. brown sugar   4 oz. fresh mushrooms, sliced
1 medium onion, chopped   1 can cream of chicken soup
3 c. hot cooked brown or wild rice

Preheat oven to 375 degrees

Wash pumpkin well and dry with paper towel.
Cut top out of pumpkin and remove seeds, cleaning inside well.
Brown hamburger and drain well. Set aside.
Sauté mushrooms and onions in same skillet until lightly browned.
Combine all ingredients and place in pumpkin.
Replace the pumpkin cap. Rub pumpkin with olive oil to coat well.
Place in a lightly greased baking pan.
Bake for 1 hour.
Serve with some of the pumpkin as you scoop out.

Sweet Potato Biscuits

Here's a hint for a quick way to get these biscuits in the oven. Microwave a large sweet potato as if you were baking it to eat. Split open to cool a bit, scoop out your cup of cooked potato, mash it a bit with a fork and you are almost there! Yes, yes I know. It isn't a pumpkin recipe, but you can easily substitute a cup of pumpkin puree for the sweet potato for a slight twist! Either way, they do turn out orange! Wink, wink!

2 c. flour
1/2 tsp. salt
1/4 c. good shortening
1 c. sweet potato, cooked and mashed
2 1/2 tsp. baking powder
1/4 c. butter
6 Tbsp. buttermilk

Preheat oven to 450 degrees
Combine all dry ingredients.
Cut in butter and shortening.
Add sweet potatoes and enough buttermilk to form soft dough.
Roll to 3/4" thick, cut with biscuit cutter.
Bake on baking sheet or in greased baking pan 12-15 minutes.

Makes 2 dozen

* 5 1/2 tsp. milk and 1/2 tsp. vinegar to sour can replace buttermilk.

It's A Pumpkin—No! It's a Cheese Ball

I love to serve this around the holidays. To make it look even more authentic, break off the stem from a small pumpkin to use as an actual stem on the cheese ball. Just wash it well, and it presses in nicely. If you plan to make these from time to time, save a few nice looking stems. They are handy to have on hand. It's such an impressive treat. I think I will make one for the Girls Knit Out group this fall. Doubt they have ever had it. Did I mention I just love the fall!

8 oz. pkg. cream cheese, softened
¼ c. crumbled Feta cheese
10 oz. sharp Cheddar cold-pack cheese spread
¼ tsp. celery salt or seed
2 finely diced green onion tops
½ c. walnuts, finely chopped
2 tsp. Worcestershire sauce
1 tsp. paprika

Blend the cheeses together until smooth.
Stir together Worcestershire sauce, celery salt or seed and onion, adding more to taste if desired. Stir into cheese mixture.
Shape into a ball and place on serving platter, cover with plastic and chill a couple hours, until firm.
Score vertical lines with back of knife to resemble a pumpkin.
Toss walnuts with the paprika.
Roll and pat to cover the surface of the cheese ball.
Place stem in top, or use a piece of a large pretzel rod for stem if you rather.
Arrange on platter with assorted crackers.

Serves 10 - 12

Pumpkin – Cranberry Coffee Cake

This jewel has been passed down by family and friends throughout the generations. A fall favorite, it is one of those coffee cakes that gets moister every day, when there is any left that is.

Baked in a cast aluminum tube pan makes a wonderful, old-fashioned coffee cake. When turned out on a wire rack and immediately flipped back onto a plate, so the top of the cake shows the uneven surface that browned slightly during baking, a sprinkle of cinnamon sugar to nestle in the cracks and dimples completes the presentation.

2 ¼ c. all-purpose flour
1 Tbsp. cinnamon
1 tsp. baking soda
½ tsp. salt
2 large eggs, at room temperature
Cinnamon/sugar to garnish
2 c. granulated sugar
1 c. solid packed pumpkin puree
½ c. canola or vegetable oil
1 c. cranberries, coarsely chopped
1 c. chopped pecans, if desired

Preheat oven to 350 degrees.
Generously grease an 8 cup Bundt pan or tube pan and dust generously with flour, shaking out excess.
In large bowl, stir together the flour, cinnamon, baking soda and salt.
In bowl of mixer at medium speed, beat the eggs until foamy. Beat in granulated sugar, pumpkin puree and oil until well blended. Add the pumpkin mixture to the flour mixture and stir just until batter forms. Do not overmix. Gently fold in cranberries and chopped pecans.
Spread evenly in the prepared pan.
Bake 50 minutes, or until toothpick comes out clean. Let cool in pan on a rack of 10 minutes. If necessary run thin knife around rim to loosen, turn out on cooling rack and cool completely.
Sprinkle with cinnamon sugar before serving.

Orange-Pumpkin Cookies

2 ½ c. flour
1 egg
½ tsp. baking soda
1 ¾ c. solid pack pumpkin
½ tsp. salt
2 Tbsp. orange juice
1 c. butter, softened
1 tsp. grated orange peel
1 c. sugar
½ c. chopped nuts
½ c. brown sugar
Orange glaze, to follow

Preheat oven to 375
Combine flour, baking soda and salt with whisk.
In mixing bowl cream butter, sugar and brown sugar until creamy.
Add egg, pumpkin, orange juice and orange peel; beat to combine.
Gradually add flour mixture, just to combine. Stir in nuts.
Drop by tablespoonful on ungreased cookie sheets.
Bake in preheated oven at 375 for 12 to 14 minutes or until edges are set.
Remove to wire rack, cool completely before spreading each cookie with
½ tsp. of orange glaze as follows.

For Orange Glaze: Combine 1 ½ cups sifted powdered sugar, 3 Tbsp. orange juice and ½ tsp. grated orange peel, mix until smooth.

Makes 4 dozen cookies

NOVEMBER—All About Giving

Mid-way into fall, November is a gorgeous month. I love the colors and crispness. It is also a bittersweet time as the holidays grow near.

I loved to clean and decorate for company that came from near and far. In this new season of my life, I find that 'I am the company,' bringing a dish to a gathering. That does not discount how blessed I feel, or how much I eat. I hold past memories dear to my heart, but the truth is, I enjoy new experiences just as much.

I will never forget the first time I experienced Thanksgiving at CJ's Cafe. The feast to provide a meal and companionship for those with neither, well, that boy just melted my heart. I was so proud to be a part of the community that worked so hard for the well-being of others. Stories were priceless, and that little fourth-grade class that came and worked alongside the adults got a life lesson that year worth its weight in gold.

Fine times. Thankful times. Giving times for sure. We all need that experience, at least once in a lifetime. I'm proud to call Spring Forrest my home, again.

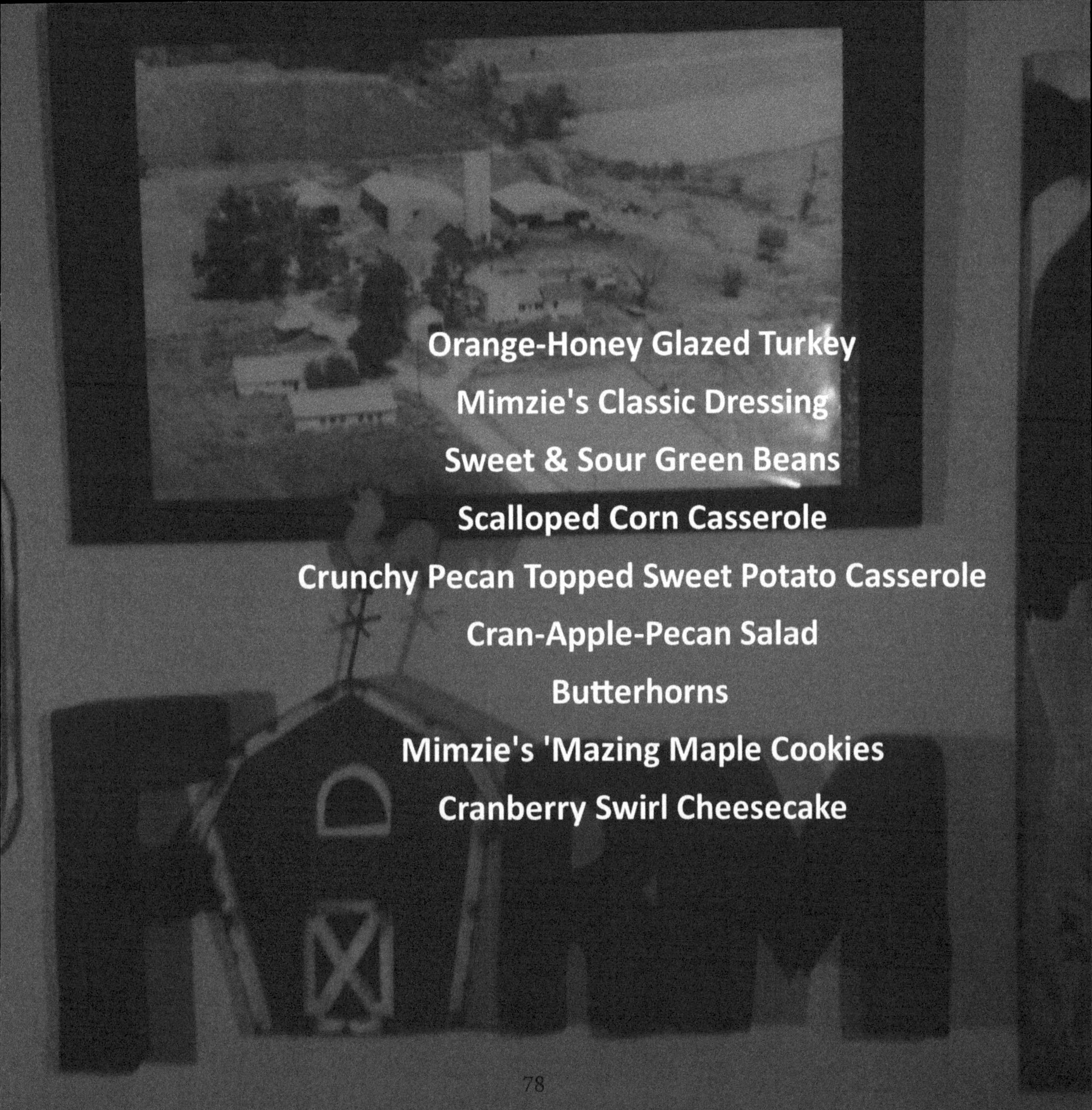

Orange-Honey Glazed Turkey

Mimzie's Classic Dressing

Sweet & Sour Green Beans

Scalloped Corn Casserole

Crunchy Pecan Topped Sweet Potato Casserole

Cran-Apple-Pecan Salad

Butterhorns

Mimzie's 'Mazing Maple Cookies

Cranberry Swirl Cheesecake

Recipes for a Memorable Thanksgiving Day

Don't we all complain about the early morning out of bed to put the turkey on for Thanksgiving company, but deep down, love every minute of it! The more to gather, the better. Our reward is the constant mix of the aromas from the oven and steam from the pots on the stovetop. I wish you a Thanksgiving Gathering that not only leaves stains on your favorite tablecloth but impressions on your heart. Enjoy every minute you labor, bite you savor and crumb you clean up. It's only once a year!

Orange-Honey Glazed Turkey

18-20 pound turkey, thawed as directed or fresh
4 tsp. sage
2 tsp. salt
2 tsp. pepper
1 orange, peeled & halved
1 onion, quartered
1 apple, quartered
1/2 c. melted butter
½ c. honey
½ c. orange juice

Prepare roaster. Wash turkey and pat dry.
Place orange, onion and apple in turkey cavity.
Combine sage, salt and pepper. Rub turkey with mixture and placing a bit in cavity as well.
Combine remaining sage mixture with butter.
Place turkey in roaster and brush with butter mixture.
Roast at 325 degrees about 5 – 5 ½ hours, until thermometer reads 170 degrees, basting every 30 minutes.
Combine orange juice and honey in saucepan. Bring to boil, then reduce to simmer for 10 minutes.
Brush over turkey when 170 degrees reached. Continue to bake 30 minutes to an hour, brushing with glaze every 15 minutes until thermometer reaches 185 degrees.
Remove and let stand 20 minutes or so before carving.
Thicken pan juices for gravy by cooking down and adding a bit of cornstarch dissolved in water, adding to boiling drippings to thicken.

Mimzie's Classic Dressing

Baked in an old crock bowl, this dressing gets a nice crust while baking. I for one can eat it the next day, cold for breakfast. My dressing is a bit different every year, but the basics keep it always good!

¾ loaf white bread, cubed and dried
¾ loaf wheat bread, cubed and dried
1 c. diced celery
1 c. diced onion
1/3 c. diced celery tops or parsley
1 c. shredded chicken
2 tsp. salt
2 tsp. pepper
2 Tbsp. rubbed sage
1 tsp. celery seed
4 eggs, slightly beaten
3 – 4 c. chicken broth
Craisins and pecans if desired

Heat oven to 350 degrees.
Generously grease large crock bowl or roaster.
In very large bowl, mix together both breads, onion, celery, tops or parsley, salt, pepper, sage and celery seed, mixing with hands to mix very well.
Add chicken, eggs and broth a cup at a time to combine. Do not over mix.
Keep adding broth until bread is wet, but not standing in liquid.
Add Craisins and pecans if desired.
Place in prepared pan, cover and bake for an hour. Uncover to let brown, continue baking until firm in center, usually about 30 more minutes. Pull up piece of bread on top to check for doneness.

Sweet & Sour Green Beans

This green bean recipe is a welcome alternative for the famous 'Green Bean Casserole' served for decades at every gathering. It is easy to make, reheats well, and your family and friends will love it. I believe Aunt Bea even served it in Mayberry!
Aunt Mildred, the other beloved Aunt!

2 – 16 oz. cans green beans
4 strips of bacon
1 large onion, chopped
1 tsp. salt
½ tsp. pepper
2 Tbsp. flour
4 Tbsp. sugar
1/3 c. vinegar

Drain beans, reserving liquid from 1 can.
Fry bacon until crisp, remove from pan and sauté onions in drippings.
Stir in flour, liquid from beans, salt & pepper, sugar and vinegar. Bring to boil.
Add green beans and simmer covered for 15 to 20 minutes.
Add crumbled bacon.
(Vinegar can be adjusted to taste. These reheat very nicely.)

Scalloped Corn Casserole

2 eggs
1 small onion, diced
1 can cream corn
1 can whole kernel corn, drained
½ c. butter, melted
1 c. sour cream
2 boxes cornbread mix

Preheat oven to 350
Grease 9x13 casserole dish or pan.
Mix all ingredients and spread evenly in prepared pan.
Bake 45 minutes until set and golden.
Serve warm.

Crunchy Pecan-Topped Sweet Potato Casserole

4 lbs. of sweet potatoes
¼ c. butter
1 c. brown sugar
½ c. evaporated milk (Milnot)

Boil potatoes until tender. Cool enough to handle and peel.
Mash potatoes, adding brown sugar, butter and evaporated milk.
Place in lightly greased casserole. Set aside.

Topping:
¾ c. brown sugar
¼ c. butter
¼ c. flour
1 c. chopped pecans

Combine all ingredients with fork to make crumble.
Spread evenly over potato mixture.
Bake in 350 oven for 45 minutes until topping is lightly browned.
This can be put together and stored in refrigerator a day ahead.

Butterhorns

Oh, if this recipe could talk! This has been a go-to recipe from the beginning to teach a new baker how to work with yeast dough. I wish taking pictures had been more readily available back in the day. The stories would be priceless. Now is the time, if you have a new baker, warm your kitchen and your heart with a lesson in Butterhorns. They may not always look the same, but somehow this forgiving recipe always creates a memory. Good thing. There's never any leftovers!

2 packages (1/4 ounce each) active dry yeast
1/3 c. warm water (110 – 115 degrees)
9 c. flour, divided
2 c. warm milk (110 – 115 degrees)
½ c. butter and ½ c. shortening
1 c. sugar
6 eggs
2 tsp. salt
4 Tbsp. butter, melted

In a large mixing bowl, dissolve yeast in water.
Add 4 cups flour, milk, butter & shortening, sugar, eggs and salt; beat for 2 minutes or until smooth.
Add enough remaining flour to form a soft dough.
Turn onto a floured surface; knead lightly.
Place in a greased bowl, turning once to coat and cover with damp cloth.
Let rise in warm place until doubled, 2-3 hours.
Punch down.
Divide into 4 to 5 pieces. Roll each piece into 9 inch circle.
Brush with melted butter. Cut each circle into 8 wedges; a pizza cutter works best.
Roll each wedge from the wide end to the point. Place on lightly greased baking sheet tip down, spacing 2" apart.
Spray waxed paper with oil and lightly cover rolls, let rise in warm place 30 – 45 minutes until doubled.
Preheat oven to 375.
Bake 12-15 minutes until lightly browned.
Remove and serve immediately or cool on wire rack.

Cran-Apple Pecan Salad

1-16 oz. bag fresh cranberries, washed
2 apples of choice, cored and quartered, peels left on
Zest one orange before peeling,
Peel and quarter orange and remove seeds
1 c. pecans or walnuts

Place above ingredients in food processor with chopper blade one at a time, pulsing to chop. Remove to large bowl and chop next ingredient.
Dissolve 1 – 3 oz. box cranberry or raspberry gelatin ½ cup boiling water.
Stir 1 c. sugar through chopped fruit and nuts.
Stir the dissolved gelatin into fruit mixture.
Cover and place in refrigerator several hours before serving.
Remove lid and stir every half hour or so.

This is not only wonderful with dinner but makes a perfect fruit salad for breakfast or snacks. You may want to double!

Cranberry Swirl Cheesecake

Our family has always been a big fan of cranberries. Year round I serve cranberry sauce with meals a couple of times a week. Mixing in a can of mandarin oranges or pineapple tidbits adds a bit of variety, and always welcome. When I created this cheesecake recipe, it quickly became a holiday favorite. Oh, I still make the traditional pumpkin pie, but everyone has that favorite recipe on hand, so I felt obligated to throw in something a bit different. Hope you enjoy it as much as we do!

*2 ¼ c. cinnamon graham cracker crumbs
1 (16 oz. can) whole cranberry sauce
3 – 8 oz. pkg. cream cheese, softened
1 Tbsp. cornstarch
1 tsp. pure vanilla extract
¼ c. butter, melted
2 tsp. cinnamon
1 c. sugar
4 large eggs, room temp

Preheat oven to 350 degrees
For the crust, combine crumbs and butter stirring well to combine.
Press in bottom and 1" up sides of lightly greased 9" springform pan.
Bake for 10 minutes. Let cool.
For the batter, start by processing cranberry sauce and cinnamon in food processor until smooth.
Beat cream cheese in mixer bowl until smooth.
Mix sugar and cornstarch together, add to cheese and beat well.
Add eggs, one at a time, continue beating after each addition on low speed.
Stir in vanilla.
Pour half of the batter in cooled crust, smoothing out evenly.
Spoon half of the cranberry mixture over batter, swirl gently with knife, careful not to break crust.
Top with remaining cheese mixture. Top with remaining cranberry mixture, gently swirling again, careful not to overmix.
Place pan on baking sheet and place in oven.
Bake at 350 degrees for 15 minutes.
Reduce heat to 325 degrees and continue baking for 1 hour and 10 minutes longer.
Remove from oven, let stand 10 minutes.
Run knife around sides of cheesecake to loosen from pan. Let cool completely before releasing sides of pan.
Chill for at least 2 hours or overnight. Remove from pan onto desired serving platter.
Garnish with a few fresh cranberries and mint leaves if desired.
*Sugar cookies, ginger snaps or desired crumbs may be used for this crust.

Mimzie's 'Mazing Maple Cookies

3 c. oats
1 c. shredded unsweetened coconut
2 2/3 c. flour
1 tsp. salt
1 tsp. cinnamon
2 c. packed light brown sugar
1 c. butter
1/2 c. maple syrup
2 Tbsp. light corn syrup
2 tsp. baking soda
1/4 c. boiling water
1 tsp. maple extract
2 c. chopped pecans

Preheat oven to 325

Line two baking sheets with parchment paper.
Combine oats, coconut, flour, salt, cinnamon and brown sugar in a bowl, whisking to blend.
Combine butter and syrups in a medium saucepan. Cook over medium heat until butter melts, stirring occasionally.
Remove from heat.
Combine baking soda and boiling water, stirring to dissolve.
Add to maple syrup mixture, stirring well.
Add maple extract.
Fold pecans into dry ingredients.
Stir maple mixture into dry ingredients to combine.
Scoop 1/4 c. size balls of dough on baking sheets about 3 inches apart. Flatten slightly with bottom of glass dipped in sugar.
Bake 18-20 minutes or until golden brown and set.
Cool 5 minutes on tray before removing to cooling rack to cool completely.

WINTER

    Just as no two snowflakes are exactly alike...we each celebrate this season in our own special way. Changes take place as the generations grow up and begin to take on the task of starting new traditions while making new memories of their own. Families move away, some sadly drift apart, but the chill in the air and the spirit of Christmas stirs our souls and bring back the kid in each of us. Travel doesn't seem so far; crowded houses are considered a blessing and no one can wait for the first sheet of Christmas cookies to cool enough to grab.

After the holidays the cold dark days seem to drag on. It is during those time that I love to put on a pot of soup and bake some rolls. With a nice yarn project on my lap, staring out the window as I work, my mind would drift off peacefully as I relive the recent houseful for the holidays.

DECEMBER—All About the Perfection of Confections

    This is to be my first Christmas since coming home to Spring Forrest and feeling settled. With that being said, invites are going out before Thanksgiving to all of my friends and family requesting time to spend with me. I have plans to host my first candy/cookie day. My kitchen is large enough to accommodate six of us while my dining room, so close by, has a harvest table that opens to set twelve places, so certainly, a lot of the finishing touches could be perfected there. I've had so much fun seeking out the recipes, old ones, familiar ones and some really unique ideas for my first annual event. At least, I hope it becomes an annual tradition.

    Now, with my freshly brewed cup of Blackberry Sage Tea and a stack of adorable invites, I'm finding a comfy chair with a nice ray of sunshine on my shoulders and getting myself busy. The second Saturday in December will be here in a blink, and I have a lot of decorating plans to decide on as well. Can't have company for Christmas without all the trimmings now, can we?

    I'm happy to share my recipes with you. I hope you find a special one that your own family will request each coming year. Calories aren't an issue if you decorate like I do. I'm certain to burn them off come January when I reluctantly pack all of my treasures away for another year.

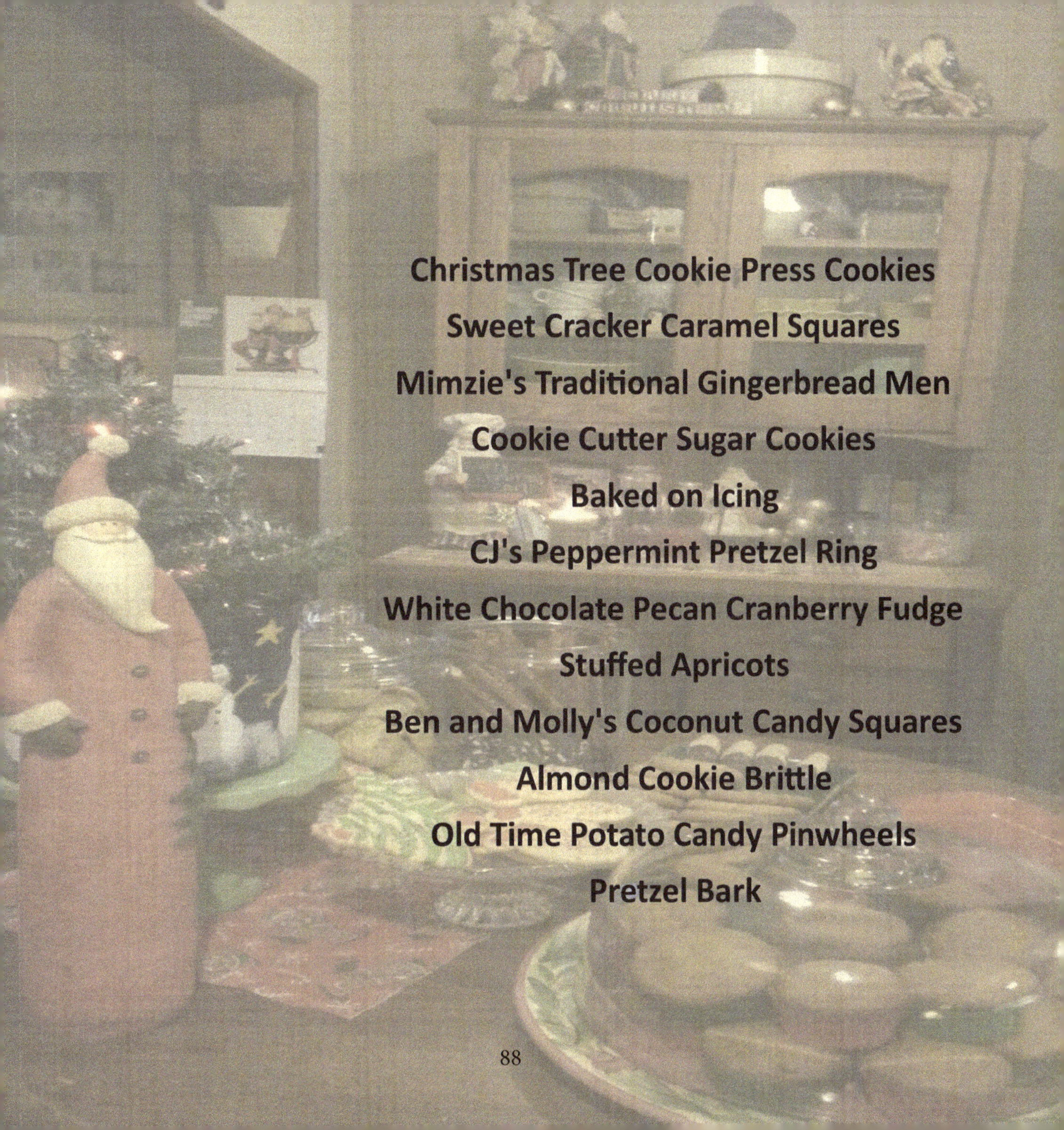

Christmas Tree Cookie Press Cookies

Sweet Cracker Caramel Squares

Mimzie's Traditional Gingerbread Men

Cookie Cutter Sugar Cookies

Baked on Icing

CJ's Peppermint Pretzel Ring

White Chocolate Pecan Cranberry Fudge

Stuffed Apricots

Ben and Molly's Coconut Candy Squares

Almond Cookie Brittle

Old Time Potato Candy Pinwheels

Pretzel Bark

Christmas Tree Cookie Press Cookies

1 c. shortening
1 c. sugar
1 tsp. pure vanilla
2 ½ c. flour
¼ tsp. cinnamon

1 – 3 oz. pkg. cream cheese
1 egg yolk
2 tsp. orange zest
½ tsp. salt

Preheat oven to 350 degrees
Cream together shortening, cream cheese and sugar.
Beat in egg yolk, vanilla and orange zest.
Whisk together flour, salt and cinnamon and add gradually to shortening mixture.
Fill cookie press with desired pattern and form on ungreased cookie sheets.
Decorate as desired.
Bake 12 – 15 minutes just until edges start to turn golden.
Remove to cooling racks at once.

Makes 6 – 7 dozen cookies

Dough can be tinted for occasion if desired.

Sweet Cracker Caramel Squares

35 good saltine crackers
1 c. light brown sugar
1 c. butter, cubed
1 1/2 tsp. pure vanilla
3/4 c. white, dark or milk chocolate chips
1/2 c. chopped nuts

Preheat oven to 350 degrees
Line jelly roll pan with parchment paper.
Place crackers over entire sheet in uniform rows, 7 x 5.

Make caramel mixture:
1 c. light brown sugar
1 c. butter, cubed
1-1/2 tsp. pure vanilla

For the caramel mixture, in heavy saucepan bring light brown sugar and butter to boil.
Once it starts to boil, turn the heat down, allowing the mixture to continue to bubble, stirring constantly continuing to cook for 5 minutes. This should produce a soft ball stage.

Final steps for assembly:
Pour hot mixture carefully over prepared crackers, not to shuffle them around. Pop in hot oven and bake for 5 minutes or until bubbly.
Remove from oven, sprinkle with chocolates and using an offset spatula, spread melted chocolate evenly over caramel mixture.
Sprinkle with nuts as desired.
Allow to cool in refrigerator for an hour. Remove from pan, peel off parchment paper and break apart.
Store in airtight container in refrigerator. Keeps for months!

Mimzie's Traditional Gingerbread Men

These were a favorite starting with Mimzie teaching little fingers to make these happy little characters, cutting hole in top to hang on the tree. The baked-on icing she came up with made it simpler, less sweet and perfect for the branches. I hope you can start a new tradition at your house, just be careful, those little ones always try the first bite, before baking. Lesson learned and never forgotten!

1/3 c. butter, softened
1 large egg
2-3/4 c. flour
¾ tsp. baking soda
2 tsp. ground ginger
¾ c. packed brown sugar
½ c. molasses
½ tsp. baking powder
¼ tsp. salt
¾ tsp. cinnamon

Preheat oven to 350 degrees when preparing cookies to bake.
Beat butter until creamy. Add sugar and beat until light and creamy.
Add egg, beating on low to blend.
Gradually mix in molasses with mixer on low speed.
Combine dry ingredients in medium bowl, stir with whisk to combine.
Add to creamed mixture, blending on low speed just to form soft dough.
Flatten and wrap in waxed paper. Chill about an hour until firm enough to handle.
Working with half of the dough at a time, roll to ¼" thickness on lightly floured surface.
Cut with desired cookie cutters and decorate with Baked on Icing as desired. (Cut a hole in top of each cookie with straw before baking if using as an ornament or plan to add ribbon).
Bake on lightly greased cookie sheet for 8 minutes.
Let stand on cookie sheet 3 minutes and remove to wire rack to cool completely.

Cookie Cutter Sugar Cookies

½ c. butter, softened
¾ tsp. pure vanilla
2 c. flour
½ tsp. salt
¾ c. sugar
1 egg
½ tsp. baking soda

Preheat oven to 375 degrees when getting closer to baking cookies. It can take a while to decorate these.
Cream together butter, sugar and vanilla until light and fluffy.
Add egg, mixing well.
Combine dry ingredients with whisk in separate bowl
Add to creamed mixture, blending well.
Dived dough into 3 parts to make easier rolling.
At this point, the dough may be tinted if desired. If too soft, refrigerate 10 minutes or so. Do not let it get too stiff.
Roll dough on lightly floured surface to about 1/4" thickness.
Cut and decorate as desired using either sugars or baked on icing recipe to follow.
Place on ungreased cookie sheets and bake 8-10 minutes, just until very lightly browned. Do not overbake.
Let stand 5 minutes before removing to wire rack to cool completely.

Baked-on Icing

2/3 c. butter   ¼ c. powdered sugar   2/3 c. flour

Beat all ingredients together until smooth.
Divide to color as desired.
Pipe onto cookie dough already cut into shapes and on cookie sheet.

CJ's Peppermint Pretzel Ring

After decorating a small tree with his favorite traditional gingerbread men cookies, CJ said he was feeling creative. Time on his hands, he decided to make his tree into a real presentation. He said he thought it needed a tree skirt, edible of course. Favorite platter at hand, and who doesn't like chocolate dipped pretzels; he quickly went to work. It was indeed a show-stopper...while it lasted, anyway! Requested each Christmas, it certainly makes the sideboard with all of the Christmas favorites a bit more special. Thank you, CJ!

1-24 oz. white almond bark candy coating
10 oz. bag large pretzels
1-6 oz. peppermint candies, crushed, or favorite chips or sprinkles

Melt coating in double boiler, stirring until smooth.
Dip pretzels to coat completely, placing on waxed paper, working with a few at time, and before set, quickly sprinkle with crushed candy or favorite sprinkle.
When set, start arranging in ring around outside rim of desired plate, overlapping slightly as you go. When circle complete, you may begin second layer in same manner, or in reverse order to complete additional layer.

White Chocolate Pecan and Cranberry Fudge

8 oz. cream cheese, room temp.
2 tsp. pure vanilla
1 c. pecan pieces
1 c. dried cranberries
2 c. powdered sugar
16 oz. white chocolate, melted and slightly cooled

Line 9" square pan with foil.
Beat cream cheese, powdered sugar and vanilla until smooth.
Add melted white chocolate, continue to mix.
Fold in dried cranberries and pecan.
Spread in pan. Refrigerate until firm.
Remove from pan, cut into 1" squares. Keep refrigerated.

Stuffed Apricots

(Filling)
3-oz. pkg. cream cheese
1 tsp. lemon juice
2 Tbsp. finely ground pecans
1 pkg. dried apricots
2 Tbsp. yogurt or milk
3 Tbsp. powdered sugar

Mix all ingredients except apricots, beating until smooth.
Slit the tip of apricot where seed removed.
Place filling in pastry bag with large open tip, insert tip in slit and squeeze to fill apricot.
Refrigerate until firm, about 30-45 minutes.

Dip
1 c. dark chocolate chips   ½ tsp. Crisco

Melt over double boiler (or in microwave), stirring until smooth.
Dip the chilled apricots, starting at the slit end, covering about half in chocolate.
Lay on waxed paper lined pan. Chill chocolate.
Serve cold. Store in refrigerator.

Ben & Molly's Coconut Candy Squares

Each year, Ben and Molly spend a couple of evenings making this amazing candy. The second night when they dip and decorate it, It's a Wonderful Life will be playing in the background. Watched over the years, time and time again, I imagine they could easily quote the next line. Holiday traditions, to so many of us, are not as much about the taste as the time spent preparing the treat. In this case, it is a win-win! They have perfected both taste and presentation. I remember watching the mail two weeks before Christmas every year, just for the arrival of their wonderful greeting! Now that I'm back in Spring Forrest, I just may ask if I can quietly watch the production, being ever so careful not to change anything about their routine. I'm just happy that I no longer have to wait on the mail!

4 c. powdered sugar
4 c. flaked coconut
3/4 c. cold mashed potatoes without any milk or butter
1 1/2 tsp. pure vanilla
1/2 tsp. salt
1 lb. good dark chocolate chips

Mix powdered sugar, coconut, potatoes, vanilla and salt well in mixing bowl on low speed to combine.
Spread into a 9" square pan, lined with foil.
Cover and chill overnight.
Remove from pan and cut into 2"x1" rectangle pieces.
Melt chocolate in top of double boiler.
Dip each piece in chocolate and place on waxed paper to harden.

For Christmas, use white chocolate melt and add sprinkles if desired or color white chocolate for occasion.

Old Time Potato Candy Pinwheels

Mimzie told of this candy every Christmas, reminiscing of the simpler times when even the basic ingredients made a delicious treat. I know she only made them about every third year or so. She said they were so rich; she didn't want anyone getting sick from eating too many and ruin a perfectly good memory. I miss her. She had such a way with words. Perhaps I'll make a batch this year for the girls at Girls Knit Out and introduce them to days gone by.

1 medium potato   1 lb. powdered sugar
½ c. peanut butter

Boil the potato until tender. Peel and mash, and while hot add powdered sugar while mashing until stiff.
Roll out into a rectangle on board dusted with powdered sugar to about 3/8" thickness.
Spread with peanut butter.
Roll up jellyroll style, starting at wide side. Cut into 1" slices.
Cover tightly to store as it dries out easily.

Almond Cookie Brittle

1 c. butter   1 c. sugar
1 tsp. salt   2 c. flour
1 c. sliced almonds
1 tsp. almond extract
Preheat oven to 350.

Cream butter, sugar, salt and almond extract.
Stir in flour until blended. Fold in nuts.
Press dough to 3/8 inch thick in a jelly roll pan.
Bake 15-20 minutes.
(Shorter time, chewier cookies longer time, crispier cookies)
Leave in pan to cool, then break apart like peanut brittle.
Store in airtight container

Pretzel Bark

2 c. good dark chocolate chips
2 c. crushed pretzels
1 c. finely crushed peppermint candy
 or   1 c. Peppermint candy chips

Place waxed paper on cookie sheet, set aside.
Melt the dark chocolate in double boiler.
Crush pretzels by pulsing in food processor or with pretzels in plastic bag and rolling pin.
When chocolate melted and smooth, stir in pretzels.
Quickly spread on waxed paper.
Top with peppermint chips or candy and press gently to hold.
Set outside for a few minutes to harden or place in refrigerator.
After completely hardened, break into pieces.
Store in airtight container. No need to keep refrigerated.
Can use nuts or white chips to replace peppermint if desired.
Decorate with sprinkles if desired.

COMING SOON

Welcome back if you are a loyal follower of my Simple Stitch series, or welcome aboard if this is your first visit! I'm so pleased that you are here.

A SIMPLE STITCH, A FAMILIAR PATTERN

Eliza's lovely shop, 'A Simple Stitch' is all a buzz! There are new finds daily since Aunt Mildred joined her, intermingling her antiques and uniques throughout the ample supply of quality yarn goods. 'Girls Knit Out' enjoy their usual Friday night gatherings while a new group of classmates set out to help 'A Snug Around the Neck' to make a difference in their community.

Wedding plans are in full swing. Slipknot Farm is evolving in many directions as it undergoes changes to usher it into a new season. There is an adventure around every corner, something always simmering on the stove at the Homestead and stories to be shared with new friends while being revisited by familiar faces.

As the weeks unfold before the wedding, history seems to be repeating itself. Is it by chance or the extra effort by family and friends making certain this rich heritage is kept alive with 'A Familiar Pattern'? While recycling the past into an unforgettable future, so many lives are enriched simply by being a part of this amazing event.

Just as some plans play out flawlessly, others take unexpected turns at the drop of a hat. So cozy up and join in as the past comes to life and futures are mapped out and once again, everyone strengthens their own Common Thread, looking back at where it all began. You, like the rest, will never want to leave.

A bit about me...

I'm still living in my century-old farmhouse in Southern Illinois. My surroundings are my inspiration. I love to share my version of Slipknot Farm when I get an opportunity. Upon the release of A Simple Stitch, A Time to Mend it was featured in our local newspapers. I knew this was an opportunity, so I invited my readers to come and experience my inspiration. An open house!

I recruited a couple of friends, family and my publisher to help me with guests. Preparing three recipes that were mentioned throughout the first novel and the sequel had the refreshments covered. Soon, the moment of truth arrived as the clock chimed noon. In anticipation, I watched as the door opened and guests continued to arrive until four. Familiar faces that brought their friends with them. It was awesome.

I enjoyed the feedback, or shall I say, compliments on my first novel, sharing the treats and giving tours of our comforting home. As an added touch, I created a make-shift 'Antiques & Uniques' with some of Aunt Mildred's finds for sale as well. A day I will never forget. It was humbling.

This cookbook has been a true labor of love, as I wanted to share even more of my inspiration, passing on recipes collected throughout the years. It was a much larger project than I had imagined. I had the vision and wanted it to be special.

That being said, I can now continue with my next novel in the series and then move on to the pre-quell. Writing is my passion. Sharing what I love is a bonus.

So I will continue to enjoy this amazing journey that God has so graciously placed before me, knowing I could not do this alone, enjoying everyone that crosses my path along the way. Who knows where this ride will take me next!

Kindly,

DebO

APPETIZERS & STARTERS

Deep Fried Zucchini	45
Eliza's Deviled Eggs	24
It's a Pumpkin - No! It's a Cheese Ball	74
Mushroom Cilantro Bites	46
Pepper Jelly	47

BEVERAGES

Lemon Melon Coolers	48
Perfect Peach Tea	25
Spring Blueberry Lemonade	38

BREADS, BISCUITS & SCONES

Apple Pecan Pull-Apart Bread	59
Blackberry Scones w/Blackberry Glaze	36
Butterhorns	82
Buttery Garlic Bread	3
Buttery Perfection Dinner Rolls	24
Calico Cornbread with Pepper Jelly	66
CJ's Country Ham Scones with Maple Butter	5
Fresh from Mimzie's Berry Patch Biscuits	36

Lilly's Beer Bread	16
Sweet Potato Biscuits	74
Uncle Ben's Mile High Biscuits	29

CAKES & PIES

Aunt Mildred's Apple Crisp with at Twist	57
Aunt Mildred's Lattice-Topped Rhubarb Pie	48
Autumn's Harvest Apple Cake	58
Banana Cupcakes	53
GGG's Unforgettable Pineapple Up-Side-Down Cake	69
Mama Simpkins Prize-winning Gourmet Texas Sheet Cake	68
Miss Willamena's Blueberry Gateau	39
Summertime Frozen Ambrosia Pie	54
Sunflower Chocolate Pie	25
Warming You Through - Winter Lemon Cake	7

CHEESECAKES

Aunt Mildred's Perfect Apple Cheesecake	58
Chocolate Glazed Cheesecake Bites	37
Cranberry Swirl Cheesecake	83

Raspberry Swirl Streusel Cheesecake 35

COFFEE CAKES & MUFFINS

Best-ever Chocolate Chip Banana Muffins 32
Blueberry Muffins CJ's Way 40
Pumpkin Cranberry Coffee cake 75
Sour Cream Coffee cake 11
Sunday Morning Early to Rise Coffee cake 65

COOKIES

Baked on Icing 90
Christmas Tree Cookie Press Cookies 89
Cinnamon-Apple-Raisin Cookies 59
Cookie Cutter Sugar Cookies 90
Easy Oatmeal Fudge Drop Cookies 54
GGG's Chewy Chocolaty Cookies 32
Mimzie's 'Mazing Maple Cookies 83
Mimzie's Traditional Gingerbread Men 90
Orange-Pumpkin Cookies 75
Snickerdoodles & Chipper-doodles 6
Toasted Almond Fingers 15

CANDIES & SWEET TREATS

Almond Cookie Brittle	92
Ben and Molly's Coconut Candy Squares	92
CJ's Peppermint Pretzel Ring	91
Cream Puffs	5
Old Time Potato Candy Pinwheels	92
Pretzel Bark	93
Stuffed Apricots	91
Sweet Cracker Caramel Squares	89
White Chocolate Pecan Cranberry Fudge	91

MAIN DISHES

Annie's Favorite Southwest Lasagna	66
Annie's Surprise Dinner-in-a-Pumpkin	73
Chicken, Rice, and Black Bean Casserole	30
CJ's All-day Country Omelet	31
Eliza's Simple Superb Chicken Salad	51
Mimzie's Fried Chicken	67
Orange-Honey Glazed Turkey	80
Smoked Pork Chops with Pepper Jelly	13
Spicy Glazed Ham	23

Uncle Ben's Famous Sausage Gravy — 29

SALADS

Cran-Apple-Pecan Salad — 82

Eliza's Crunchy Cole Slaw — 52

Greek Bowtie Pasta Salad — 23

SIDES

CJ's Calico Beans with Pineapple — 14

CJ's Cafe Special Zucchini Patties — 52

Crunchy Pecan-Topped Sweet Potato Casserole — 81

Mimzie's Classic Dressing — 80

Papa's Fried Cabbage and Noodles — 46

Scalloped Corn Casserole — 81

Sweet & Sour Green Beans — 81

SOUPS

Cabbage Patch Soup — 45

Caroline's Abundant Harvest Squash Soup — 73

Cheeseburger Soup — 3

Eliza's Crowd-Pleasing Chicken & Noodles
    with Gnocchi — 12

Great-Grandma's Potato Soup — 4

CPSIA information can be obtained
at www.ICGtesting.com
Printed in the USA
LVHW021715220519
618167LV00001B/3/P